Penguin Education

Childhood in Society

Two Worlds of Childhood
Urie Bronfenbrenner

Two Worlds
of Childhood
US and USSR
Urie Bronfenbrenner

Penguin Education

Penguin Education
A Division of Penguin Books Ltd,
Harmondsworth, Middlesex, England
Penguin Books Australia Ltd,
Ringwood, Victoria, Australia

First published in the US by Russell Sage Foundation, 1970
First published in Great Britain by Allen & Unwin, 1971
First published by Penguin Education, 1974
Copyright © Russell Sage Foundation, 1970, 1971, 1974
Made and printed in Great Britain by Hazell Watson & Viney Ltd

Acknowledgments

THIS BOOK is the outgrowth of three sets of scientific adventures. The first is a research project, entitled "Cross-Cultural Studies in Child Rearing," conducted for the past five years under a grant from the National Science Foundation. Fundamentally, this volume is the product and by-product of that endeavor. It has provided the basic comparative data. More importantly, it was the exposure to patterns of upbringing in other cultures, especially in the U.S.S.R., which alerted me to the impressive power—and even greater potential—of models, peers, and group forces in influencing the behavior and development of children. Finally, it was this comparative research which sensitized me to the disruptive trends in the process of socialization in American society, and spurred involvement in the design of counteractive programs. It is all of these matters which make up the body of the present work. Thus, in the last analysis, not only many of the facts, but many more of the ideas presented in this volume derived from cross-cultural research. I am especially indebted to my colleagues engaged in that effort, Edward C. Devereux, Jr., Robert R. Rodgers, George J. Suci, as well as the members of a devoted technical staff, Kathryn Dowd, Elizabeth Kiely, Mary McGinnis, Jaya Narayanamurti, Carol Theodore, Jancis Smithells, and Gitta Berstein.

The second scientific adventure was the offspring of the first; namely, a series of seven visits to the U.S.S.R., which have enabled the author to acquire the background for, develop, and finally carry out the field observations, interviews, and experiments on which the analysis of Soviet methods of upbringing and their effects is based. The writer made his first trip to the Soviet Union in 1960 as one of several scientists asked by the American Psychological Association to assess Soviet work in this field.* The second journey was made in 1961 as a member of an official United States exchange mission in the field of public health. These visits provided an opportunity to arrange for a scientific exchange between Cornell University and the Institute of Psychology in Moscow. This exchange has made possible a series of five visits, ranging in length from a few weeks to several months, in the course of which the more systematic aspects of the research were carried out. These field trips were made possible by grants from the National Science Foundation, the Russell Sage Foundation, and the Committee on Soviet Studies of Cornell University.

There is no adequate way of acknowledging the generous cooperation and hospitality extended to the author by both the Institute of Psychology and its parent organization, the Academy of Pedagogical Sciences. Special thanks are due to Dr. A. A. Smirnov, Director of the Institute of Psychology; Dr. A. N. Leontiev, Chairman of the newly established Faculty of Psychology at the University of Moscow; Dr. A. V. Zaporozhets, Director of the Institute of Preschool Education; Dr. G. S. Kostyuk, Director of the Kiev Institute of Psychology; and, in particular, Dr. L. I. Bozhovich, Head of the Laboratory of Upbringing in the Moscow Institute, and all the staff members of that Laboratory, notably I. G. Dimanshtain, E. S. Makhlakh, M. Z. Neimark, N. F. Prokina, E. I. Savonko, and S. G. Yakobson, who despite heavy research commitments of their own, gave so generously of their knowledge and assistance. Similar indebtedness is expressed to colleagues in the Academy of Pedagogical Sciences who devoted many hours to answering endless questions and arranging for innumerable visits to nurseries, schools, Pioneer palaces, camps, and other children's facilities. To the extent that the author has achieved some understanding of Soviet methods of upbringing, he owes it to the patience and pedagogical skill of leading Soviet educators, notably Professor V. Gmurman, M. N. Kolmakova, L. E. Novikova, B. E. Shirvindt, and especially E. G. Kostyashkin, Z. A. Malkova, and E. M. Sokolov.

* Cf. Raymond Bauer (ed.), *Some Views of Soviet Psychology* (Washington, D.C.: American Psychological Association, 1962).

The third set of adventures had to do less with research than its implications. The results of our cross-cultural studies called attention to problems of child rearing in American society of sufficient gravity to require some programmatic action. As a result, the author became heavily involved in the development of Project Head Start, serving as a member of the committee which designed and gave professional direction to this national program. The last two chapters of this volume had their beginnings as a document prepared at the request of Project Head Start for presentation at a conference of researchers and practitioners concerned with the development of intervention programs. Many of the ideas in that document emerged from the experience of the author as a member of the Head Start Planning Committee. In addition, appreciation is expressed to the following colleagues with whom I have discussed ideas presented in Part II of this volume, and some of whom have read and generously commented on earlier drafts of the manuscript: Robert Aldrich. Albert Bandura, Leonard Berkowitz, David Cohen, James S. Coleman, Robert Cooke, Nicholas Hobbs, David Hoffman, Melvin Kohn, John Lear, John Marcham, Walter Mischel, Francis Palmer, Thomas Pettigrew, Julius Richmond, Jules Sugarman, and Edward Zigler.

Finally, the author owes much to his friend and colleague John C. Condry, Jr. In addition to taking responsibility for editing the final draft for publication, throughout the preparation of the manuscript he gave generously of his knowledge and social concern. His searching questions, constructive criticism, and hard-headed encouragement did much to enrich the contents of this book and bring it to completion. Many of his suggested additions have been incorporated in the text.

The writing of this book was made possible by a grant from the Russell Sage Foundation. I am especially indebted to Orville G. Brim, Jr., President of the Foundation, for his encouragement, firmness, and patience in seeing this volume through to the light of day. And last but not least, I am deeply indebted to Lovetta Cahill for typing the manuscript of this book, not once, but twenty times.

Pictures generously provided by Soviet colleagues appear on pages 24 (*top and bottom*), 25 (*middle*), 27 (*bottom*), 52 (*top and bottom*), and 53. The rest of the photographs were taken by the author. He is also responsible for the translations of all citations from Russian sources. The transliteration system used is that employed by the *Current Digest of the Soviet Press*. Revised sections of various chapters have previously appeared in published articles by the author in *The Saturday Review* (Science and Humanity Supplement), *The American Psychologist*, *The Canadian Journal of Behavioral Sciences*, the research supplement to *Religious Education*, and as a chapter in *The Role and Status of Women in the Soviet Union*, edited by Donald R. Brown and published by Teachers College Press, Columbia University, in 1968.

Contents

INTRODUCTION   *A Criterion for Two Cultures*   1

PART I   THE MAKING OF THE NEW SOVIET MAN   5

CHAPTER 1   Upbringing in the Soviet Family   7
Patterns of Maternal Care
Values and Techniques of Discipline

CHAPTER 2   Upbringing in Collective Settings   15
Techniques of Upbringing in Preschool Centers
Upbringing in Soviet Schools

CHAPTER 3   The Psychological Implications of
Soviet Methods of Upbringing   70
The Effects of Affection and its Withdrawal
Father Absence and the Mother-Centered Family
Collective Upbringing in Social Psychological
   Perspective
Portents of Change

PART II   CHILD REARING IN AMERICA:
PAST, PRESENT, AND FUTURE   93

CHAPTER 4   The Unmaking of the American Child   95
An Outmoded Past
The Split Society
Adults vs. Peers
Children and Television
The Impact of Peers
The Impact of Television

Looking Backward
Looking Forward

CHAPTER 5   Principles and Possibilities   120
Conserving Biological Potential
The Potency of Models
Social Reinforcement
Intensive Relationships
Group Forces
Superordinate Goals
Soviet Upbringing Revisited

CHAPTER 6   From Science to Social Action   152
The Classroom
The School
The Family
The Neighborhood
The Larger Community

Source Notes   167
Index   187

Introduction

A Criterion for Two Cultures

How CAN WE judge the worth of a society? On what basis can we predict how well a nation will survive and prosper? Many indices could be used for this purpose, among them the Gross National Product, the birth rate, crime statistics, mental health data, etc. In this book we propose yet another criterion: *the concern of one generation for the next.* If the children and youth of a nation are afforded opportunity to develop their capacities to the fullest, if they are given the knowledge to understand the world and the wisdom to change it, then the prospects for the future are bright. In contrast, a society which neglects its children, however well it may function in other respects, risks eventual disorganization and demise.

In this book, we shall explore the "concern of one generation for the next" in the two most powerful nations of our time, the Soviet Union and the United States. We shall examine what each country does for and with its children both intentionally and, perhaps, unintentionally. Then, drawing upon existing research and theory in the behavioral sciences, we shall ask what are, or might be, the consequences of the modes of treatment we observe; that is, what values and patterns of behavior are being developed in the new generation in each society. Finally, we shall look into the possibilities for introducing constructive changes in the process as it is taking place in our own country. In pursuing this last objective, we shall draw even more extensively on available resources of behavioral science to identify what we know of the forces affecting the development of human behavior, the principles on which the forces operate, and how these principles might be exploited by our social institutions in a manner consistent with our values and traditions.

In the language of behavioral science, this volume is concerned with the process of *socialization*, the way in which a child born into a given society becomes a social being—a member of that society. It should be clear that being socialized is not necessarily the same as being civilized. Nazi youth were also products of a socialization process. The example is an instructive one, for it reminds us that the family is not the only possible agent of upbringing. The process typically begins in the home but does not end there. The outside world also has major impact, as the child becomes exposed to a succession of persons, groups, and institutions, each of which imposes its expectations, rewards, and penalties on the child and thus contributes to shaping the development of his skills, values, and patterns of behavior.

Accordingly, in our comparative study of socialization in the Soviet Union and the United States, we shall be examining the process as it occurs in a series of social contexts beginning with the family but then proceeding to other settings such as preschool centers, children's groups, classrooms, schools, neighborhoods, communities, and, indeed, the nation as a whole.

Our selection of the Soviet Union as the object of paired comparison was not dictated by considerations of power politics but by those of social science. We wished to profit from the contrasting perspective provided by a society which differs substantially from our own in the process and context of socialization but at the same time faces similar problems as an industrialized nation with highly developed systems of technology, education, and mass communication. In terms of socialization, the major difference between the two cultures lies in the localization of primary responsibility for the upbringing of children. In the United States, we ordinarily think of this responsibility as centered in the family, with the parents playing the decisive part as the agents of child rearing, and other persons or groups outside the family serving at most in secondary or supplementary roles. Not so in the Union of Soviet Socialist Republics. The difference is nowhere better expressed than in the following passage from one of the most influential Soviet publications in this sphere: *A Book for Parents* by Anton Semyonovich Makarenko, an eminent educator whose methods for rehabilitating juvenile delinquents in the nineteen-twenties and -thirties became the primary basis for the techniques of collective upbringing currently employed in all Soviet nurseries, schools, camps, children's institutions, and youth programs. In this volume, which came to be regarded as a guide to ideal Soviet family life, Makarenko defined the role of the family as follows:

Our family is not a closed-in collective body, like the bourgeois family. It is an organic part of Soviet society, and every attempt it makes to build up its own experience independently of the moral demands of society is bound to result in a disproportion, discordant as an alarm bell.

Our parents are not without authority either, but this authority is only the reflection of social authority. In our country the duty of a father toward his children is a particular form of his duty toward society. It is as if our society says to parents:

You have joined together in goodwill and love, rejoice in your children, and expect to go on rejoicing in them. That is your own personal affair and concerns your own personal happiness. But in this happy process you have given birth to new people. A time will come when these people will cease to be only a joy to you and become independent members of society. It is not at all a matter of indifference to society what kind of people they will be. In handing over to you a certain measure of social authority, the Soviet state demands from you correct upbringing of future citizens. Particularly it relies on a certain circumstance arising naturally out of your union—on your parental love.

If you wish to give birth to a citizen and do without parental love, then be so kind as to warn society that you wish to play such an underhanded trick. People brought up without parental love are often deformed people. . . .[1]

Nor is the family the sole or even the principal delegate of the society for the upbringing of children. Such primary responsibility is vested in still another social structure, the *children's collective*, defined as "a group of children united in common, goal-oriented activity and the communal organization of this activity."[2] As we shall see, such collectives constitute the basic structural units in all Soviet programs designed for the care or education of children.

The first difference, then, between the United States and the Soviet Union in the way in which children are socialized lies in the contrast between a family- versus a collective-centered system of child rearing. But, of course, the family is not the only context of upbringing in American society. Children's groups also exist in the United States. But unlike their more formalized Soviet counterparts, they are more fluid, and relatively independent of the adult society.

Accordingly, in our comparative study, we shall focus major attention on similarities and differences in two principal contexts of socialization—the family and the children's group.

We begin with a consideration of the process of upbringing in the Soviet Union.

PART I

THE MAKING
OF THE NEW SOVIET MAN

To DATE, *no systematic studies of methods of child rearing have been carried out in the Soviet Union either by Soviet or non-Soviet investigators. The generalizations which follow are based on field notes of observations and interviews made by the author as a visiting scientist on seven different occasions from 1960 to 1967. Over the course of these visits, which ranged in length from two weeks to three months, opportunities were provided, through the courtesy of the Academy of Pedagogical Sciences, to observe and talk with children and adults in a variety of settings, including nurseries, kindergartens, regular schools, boarding schools, and the so-called schools of the prolonged day, as well as Pioneer palaces, camps, parks, and other community facilities for children and parents. In addition, particularly after the first one or two trips, there developed informal opportunities to become acquainted with Soviet family life. The presence of our own children on three of these visits not only increased such contacts considerably, but also set in high relief the contrasts between Soviet and American modes of upbringing both within and outside the family.*

Although some observations were made in rural areas in the Russian, Ukrainian, and Georgian republics, and in the Asian republics of Uzbekistan and Kazakstan, the great bulk of the field work was done in several large cities in various parts of the U.S.S.R., specifically Moscow, Leningrad, Kiev, Odessa, Tallin, Tbilisi, Tashkent, and Alma-Ata.

1

Upbringing in the Soviet Family

THE DESCRIPTIONS which follow are drawn both from field data and from published manuals on child care. Although the latter have wide circulation throughout the Union of Soviet Socialist Republics, with translations published in the languages of the several republics, the observations were essentially limited to Russian-speaking families in and around large metropolitan centers.

We begin with a discussion of parental treatment in infancy and early childhood.

Patterns of Maternal Care

In this sphere, differences between Russian and American practices are most apparent in three areas.

PHYSICAL CONTACT

Russian babies receive substantially more physical handling than their American counterparts. To begin with, breast feeding is highly recommended and virtually universal. And even when not being fed, Russian babies are still held much of the time. The nature of this contact is both highly affectionate and restricting. On the one hand, in comparison with American babies, the Russian child receives considerably more hugging, kissing, and cuddling. On the other hand, the infant is held more tightly and given little opportunity for freedom of movement or initiative. Manuals on child care, prepared by the Academy of Pedagogical Sciences, frequently inveigh against this practice. Witness the following excerpt:

> There are still mothers who, when the child is not asleep, never allow him to remain in his bed but continually hold him in their arms. They even cook holding the child with the left arm. Such a position is very harmful to the child, since it leads to curvature of the spine.[1]

SOLICITOUSNESS

The mobility and initiative of the Soviet child are further limited by a concerted effort to protect him from discomfort, illness, and injury. There is much concern about keeping him warm. Drafts are regarded as especially dangerous. Once the child begins to crawl or walk, there is worry lest he hurt himself or wander into dangerous territory. For example, children in the park are expected to keep in the immediate vicinity of the accompanying adult, and when our youngsters—aged nine and four—would run about the paths, even within our view, kindly citizens of all ages would bring them back by the hand, often with a reproachful word about our lack of proper concern for our children's welfare.

DIFFUSION OF MATERNAL RESPONSIBILITY

The foregoing example highlights another distinctive feature of Russian upbringing, the readiness of other persons besides the child's own mother to step into a maternal role. This is true not only for relatives, but even for complete strangers. For example, it is not uncommon, when sitting in a crowded public conveyance, to have a child placed on your lap by a parent or guardian. Strangers strike up acquaintances with young children as a matter of course, and are immediately identified by the accompanying adult or by the child himself as "*dyadya*" [uncle] or "*tyotya*" [auntie].

Nor is the nurturant role limited to adults. Older children of both sexes show a lively interest in the very young and are competent and comfortable in dealing with them to a degree almost shocking to a Western observer. I recall an incident which occurred on a Moscow street. Our youngest son—then four—was walking briskly a pace or two ahead of us when from the opposite direction there came a company of teenage boys. The first one no sooner spied Stevie than he opened his arms wide and, calling *"Ai malysh!"* [Hey, little one!], scooped him up, hugged him, kissed him resoundingly, and passed him on to the rest of the company, who did likewise, and then began a merry children's dance, as they caressed him with words and gestures. Similar behavior on the part of any American adolescent male would surely prompt his parents to consult a psychiatrist.

Given this diffusion of nurturant behavior toward children, it is hardly surprising that Soviet youngsters exhibit less anxiety than their American age-mates when their mother leaves them in the care of another person or in a nursery. Such delegation of the care of the child is, of course, standard practice in the U.S.S.R., a nation of working mothers in which 48 per cent of all age-eligible women are in the labor force. But before turning to methods of upbringing outside the family, we must consider another aspect of parental child rearing, values and techniques of discipline.

Values and Techniques of Discipline

It would be a mistake to conclude that the affection and solicitousness that Russians, in particular Russian mothers, lavish on children imply permissiveness or indulgence with respect to conduct. On the contrary, much emphasis is placed, no less by parents than by professional educators, on the development of such traits as obedience [*poslushanie*] and self-discipline [*distsiplinirovannost*].

What is meant concretely by these terms? For an answer we may turn to the authoritative volume, *Parents and Children,* prepared by a group of specialists from the Academy of Pedagogical Sciences with the aim of "helping parents to bring up their children properly so that they can grow up to be worthy citizens of our socialist nation."[2] In a chapter on discipline, we read the following:

> What is necessary and possible to demand of young children? First of all, a child must be *obedient* toward his parents and other adults, and treat them with respect. . . . The child must fulfill requests that adults make of him—this is the first thing the child must be taught. The child must fulfill the demands of his elders. In following the orders, instructions, and advice of grownups, the child manifests obedience. By becoming accustomed to obey from early childhood, to react to the demands of adults as something compulsory, the child will begin successfully to fulfill later demands made of him in family and school.[3]

But to obey is not enough; the child must also develop *self-discipline*. On this score, our manual speaks as follows:

> It is necessary as early as possible to develop in the young child an active, positive relation to the demands of adults, the desire to act in accordance with these demands, to do that which is necessary. Herein lies the great significance of our efforts in developing conscious self-discipline, indeed its very elements. Every person, including the young school-age child, will better, more quickly, and more joyously fulfill demands and rules once he has a desire to do so.[4]

In other words, in the parlance of Western psychology, self-discipline is internalized obedience—fulfilling the wishes of adults not as commands from without but as internally motivated desires.

A more recent work by one of the Soviet Union's most popular writers on child rearing, I. A. Pechernikova (the first edition of 150,000 copies sold out in a few months), reiterates much the same idea and then poses a critical question.

> Obedience in young children provides the basis for developing that most precious of qualities: self-discipline. Obedience in adolescents and older school children—this is the effective expression of their love, trust, and respect

toward parents and other adult family members, a conscious desire to acknowledge their experience and wisdom. This is an important aspect of preparing young people for life in a Communist society. We shall be asked: what about developing independence [*samostoyatelnost*] in children? We shall answer: if a child does not obey and does not consider others, then his independence invariably takes ugly forms. Ordinarily this gives rise to anarchistic behavior, which can in no way be reconciled with laws of living in Soviet society. Where there is no obedience, there is no self-discipline; nor can there be normal development of independence. Training in obedience is an essential condition for developing the ability of self-discipline.[5]

We quote at some length from these contemporary Soviet educators for several reasons. First, Soviet books on upbringing are widely read and taken very seriously by parents, teachers, and others engaged in work with children. Indeed, the interest extends beyond those directly concerned, since upbringing [*vospitanie*] is virtually a national hobby in the U.S.S.R. Daily newspapers frequently carry articles and letters on the subject, public lectures on the topic are widely attended, and questions of upbringing constitute a common subject of conversation among parents and non-parents alike.

Second, consistent with the foregoing statements, the passages cited present in more succinct form ideas frequently heard in conversations with Soviet parents, teachers, child-care workers, and the general public.

Third, parents, professionals, and people in general, when dealing with children, often act in accord with these stated convictions; that is, they actively strive to develop in children the traits of obedience and self-discipline described in the passages quoted.

Fourth, as we shall see, these efforts are not without success; many Soviet children do exhibit in their behavior the qualities so strongly recommended and admired by professional educators.

Finally, as we shall see also, the dilemma of obedience ver-

sus independence, which Pechernikova poses and then so readily resolves, at least at the ideological level, is likewise manifest
in the behavior of Soviet youngsters, and may present problems
for Soviet society in the light of changing educational, social,
and economic needs.

But before considering the products of Soviet upbringing it
is necessary to acquaint ourselves with the methods employed
for achieving the stated goals. Once again we begin by examining recommended practices. The treatment of this subject in
Pechernikova's book, which is the most recent at our disposal, is
typical of its many predecessors. In her chapter on "How to
Develop Obedience," Pechernikova recommends the following
as the method of choice.

> The development of obedience is especially fostered by
> a brief and precise explanation to the child of the reason
> why he should behave himself in the given fashion and not
> otherwise. In pedagogy, we call this the method of persua-
> sion.[6]

Second only to persuasion in its presumed effectiveness is
the use of encouragement and praise [*pooshchrenie*], but such
techniques "should be employed only when necessary." For example, if a child is already doing well in school and is following
the rules of conduct, he should not be praised for it.

> The method of encouragement and praise should be used
> only in those cases when, under the influence of the
> teacher, the parents, or one's friends, the child is striving
> to correct faults of character, to become better organized,
> to begin to obey his elders.[7]

Finally, Pechernikova takes up the question of how to punish
disobedience. First of all, she sounds the primary proscription
of Soviet experts on upbringing: "the inadmissability of physical punishment," a measure which is viewed not merely as in-
effective but harmful. However, after inveighing against this
particular form of discipline for seven pages, Pechernikova
warns against the opposite extreme, "the denial of any form of
punishment whatsoever, on grounds of liberalism and spon-
taneity in child rearing."[8] The so-called method of natural con-

sequences, which allows the child to learn by touching the hot samovar and burning himself, is to be vigorously rejected.

We cannot risk our children's future by allowing their upbringing to be determined by spontaneous drift. The school and the parents [note the order] must hold the reins of upbringing in their own hands and take all measures necessary to insure that children obey their elders.[9]

What measures are these? On first glance, we recognize familiar phrases, "reprimand," "dressing down," "deprivation of privileges," that is, the usual armamentarium of frustrated parents everywhere. But a more careful reading reveals a special emotional tone somewhat alien to present-day parental practices, especially recommended ones, in our own country, but possibly reminiscent of an earlier era. Witness the following examples:

A "talking-to" [involves] a brief but sharp evaluation of the behavior of the disobedient child including an expression of one's own indignation at such behavior. Moreover, after giving the reprimand, one should not permit himself to resume his usual affectionate manner with the child, even when the parent feels that the youngster has genuinely repented. For a period of time it is necessary to remain pointedly reserved with the child and somewhat cold, thereby showing him that his disobedience has hurt the adult. This measure turns out to be very effective and in most instances gives a palpable result. . . . Depriving the child of the adult's companionship in enjoyable activity as a punishment for disobedience is also a very effective means of influence.

For example, a mother says to her son: "Once again you disobeyed me by not coming home on time. Now I no longer wish to finish the chess match we began yesterday. It is even unpleasant for me to look at you." For the rest of the evening, she confines herself only to cold responses to her son's questions. About the same behavior toward the boy is shown by his father.

Sometimes the parents can resort to an even more severe method of punishment: for a period of time to cease talking to the child entirely. For example, a daughter not only disobeyed her mother by refusing to change her ridiculous hair-do but allowed herself to hurt her mother's feelings by a harsh word. The latter said nothing, but cast a reproving glance, showed by all her appearance how deeply insulted she was, and refrained from speaking with her daughter for several hours.[10]

Students of Western research on parent-child relationships will recognize this pattern as a classic example of discipline through what has been called "withdrawal of love." Shortly, we shall review available evidence on the effects of this parental technique. For the moment, we must turn to the prior question of the extent to which Soviet families actually employ the methods recommended to them by professional educators.

Here we can rely only on the informal observations and interviews conducted primarily with urban professional families but also including more casual contacts with working-class parents and children in public conveyances, parks, recreation centers, and other public places. In general, the field notes indicate considerable correspondence between practice and precept, especially among professional families. Less-cultured parents do on occasion resort to physical punishment, and are less likely to engage in reasoning and persuasion. But what most differentiates Russian parents from their American counterparts is the emotional loading of the parent-child relationship, both in its positive and negative aspects. On the one hand, both adults and children in the U.S.S.R. are more demonstrative toward each other. On the other hand, any departure from proper behavior evokes from the parent a curtailment of this demonstrativeness. By gesture, word, intonation, or eloquent silence the parent is quick to convey his emotional wound. The child is made to feel not so much that his behavior was wrong as that he himself was ungrateful and had betrayed an affectional bond.

This same principle of discipline through withdrawal of emotional support turns out to be central in the second major context in which upbringing takes place for the Soviet child—the children's collective.

2

Upbringing in Collective Settings

ALTHOUGH in the Soviet Union the use of communal facilities for the rearing of children is as old as the Soviet government itself, collective upbringing received its greatest expansion following the Twentieth Party Congress in 1956, which called not only for the expansion of existing institutions, such as nurseries and kindergartens, but also for the introduction of the so-called schools of the new type—the *"internats"* or boarding schools, and the "schools of the prolonged day," which offer essentially the same program as the boarding schools, except that the pupils go home at about six in the evening and return early the next morning.

The present scope of these programs can be gleaned from the following summary figures. Over 10 per cent of all Soviet children under two years of age are currently enrolled in public nurseries. The corresponding percentage for children between three and six years of age who attend preschool institutions is about 20 per cent. Approximately 5 per cent of all school-age children—i.e., those seven years old and older—are enrolled in boarding schools and "schools of the prolonged day."*

* For a more detailed account of the development of institutions of communal upbringing in the U.S.S.R., including available enrollment figures, see Urie Bronfenbrenner, "The Changing Soviet Family," in Donald R. Brown (ed.), *The Role and Status of Women in the Soviet Union* (New York: Teachers College Press, Columbia University, 1968). Although in his 1956 address, Nikita Khruschev predicted "the education of all children in boarding schools," his successors have markedly reduced further expansion of this type of institution in favor of the cheaper and more popular extended-day schools.

In this nursery in Uzbekistan, as in Moscow, the raised playpens provide for face-to-face interaction with the staff.

Nursery children play on an outdoor playground near Moscow.

For all of these institutions, the stated aim is to provide the child, from early infancy onward, with the physical, psychological, and social conditions regarded as necessary for his full development but not readily available in his own home. In accordance with this aim, priority in admission is given primarily to children from families in which one parent is absent or away for long periods of time, or where the parents work on different shifts. Infants may be entered at three months of age.

What is the nature of the methods of child rearing employed in these collective settings? The following account is based on observations in some thirty centers visited by the author in various parts of the U.S.S.R.

Techniques of Upbringing in Preschool Centers

Training in the first year of life involves two major features. The first is early experience in collective living. The infants are placed in group playpens with six to eight children in each. To permit face-to-face interaction between staff members and children the pens are raised on legs, the one for the three-to-six-month-olds being higher than that for the near-toddlers. At these age levels, there is one "upbringer" for every four charges.

The second core principle of upbringing is the so-called *regime*. Each child is on what a Western psychologist would view as a series of reinforcement schedules; that is, the upbringer spends a specified amount of time with him in stimulating and training sensory-motor functions. For example, at the earliest age levels, she will present a brightly colored object, moving it to and fro to encourage following. A bit later, the object is brought nearer and moved slowly forward to induce the infant to move toward it. Still later, the child is motivated to pull himself up by the barred sides of the playpen to assume a standing position. And infants learn to stand in such playpens not only in Moscow, but 2,000 miles away in Soviet Asia as well. The children in the picture at the top of page 16 are Uzbeks.

From the very beginning, considerable emphasis is given to the development of self-reliance, so that by eighteen months of age the children are expected to have completed bowel and bladder training and are already learning more complex skills such as dressing themselves. Physical activity outdoors is encouraged and it is usually followed by rest, with windows wide open and the smallest children swaddled in thick quilts.

During the first year of life, especial attention is focused on language training. The following passage from the official manual on the preschool program provides an accurate summary of our own observations:

> The upbringer exploits every moment spent with the child for the development of speech. In order that the infant learn to discriminate and understand specific words, the upbringer speaks to him in short phrases, emphasizes by her intonation the main words in a given sentence, pauses after speaking to the child, and waits for him to do what was asked. It is important that the words coincide with the

The umbrella shade is a common feature in Russian nurseries.

moment when the child engages in the action, looks at the object which the adult has named, or is watching a movement or activity being performed by the adult. The speech of the upbringer should be emotional and expressive, and should reflect her loving, tender relation to the child.

In activities with children of this age, the upbringer develops the understanding of speech and enriches the children's impressions. Toward this end she carries the baby to different objects and shows him large colorful sound-making and wind-up toys; with children eight to nine months of age, she encourages them to pick out from a collection of many toys the one which she names; in order to acquaint the child with names of adults and other children she conducts games of hide-and-seek.

In order that the child can learn the words associated with certain actions ("Clap your hands," "Goodbye," "Give

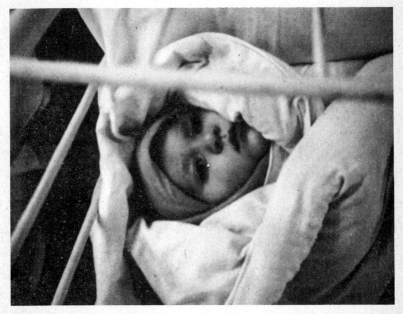

An infant is prepared for a rest on the veranda.

me your hand," "So-o big," etc.), she teaches these actions, accompanying them with the appropriate words. The up- bringer encourages the child to duplicate sounds which he already knows how to pronounce, as well as new ones, and structures his babbling and imitation of simple syllables.[1]

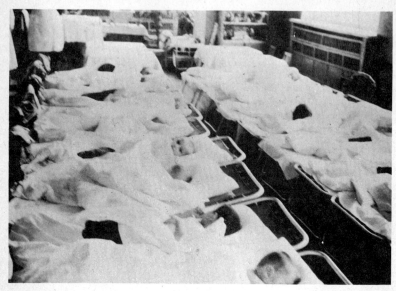

Babies nap on cots with the windows open.

Music-making is a cooperative venture.

The development of speech becomes the vehicle for developing social behavior. Thus in speaking of the nine- to twelve-months age level, the manual states:

It is important to cultivate in the baby a positive attitude toward adults and children. At this age the child's need to relate to the adults around him increases. Interest develops in what others are doing. Sometimes children of this age play together: they throw balls into the same basket, roll downhill one after the other, smile at each other, call to one another. If the upbringer is not sufficiently attentive to the children, negative relations may arise among them; for example, the result of the attempt by one child to take a toy held by another.[2]

How does the upbringer respond to such expressions of selfishness? The following example from our field notes is typical of a number of observations.

Kolya started to pull at the ball Mitya was holding. The action was spotted by a junior staff member who quickly scanned the room and then called out gaily: "Children, come look! See how Vasya and Marusya are swinging their teddy bear together. They are good comrades." The two offenders quickly dropped the ball to join others in observing the praised couple, who now swung harder than ever.

Nor is such cooperation left to chance. From the very beginning stress is placed on teaching children to share and to engage in joint activity. Frequent reference is made to common ownership: *"Moe eto nashe; nashe moe"* [mine is ours; ours is mine]. Collective play is emphasized. Not only group games, but special complex toys are designed which require the cooperation of two or three children to make them work. Music becomes an exercise in social as well as sensory-motor articulation. As soon as children are able to express themselves, they are given training in evaluating and criticizing each other's behavior from the point of view of the group. Gradually, the adult begins to withdraw from the role of leader or coordinator in order to forge a "self-reliant collective," in which the children cooperate and discipline themselves, at meal times and in play activities, too. As is apparent in some of the photographs, play often takes the form of role-playing in real-life social situations, which gradually increase in complexity (e.g., taking care of baby, shopping, in the doctor's office, at school). Beginning in the second year of

Most play activities involve sharing.

Children are expected to behave at table even without their upbringers.

nursery and continuing through kindergarten, children are expected to take on ever-increasing communal responsibilities, such as helping others, serving at table, cleaning up, gardening, caring for animals, and shovelling snow. The effects of these socializing experiences are reflected in the youngster's behavior, with many children giving an impression of self-confidence, competence, and camaraderie.

Upbringing in Soviet Schools

In the Soviet Union, children enter school proper at the age of seven. Throughout the U.S.S.R., school opens on the same day, September 1, which is a day of national celebration. Through the last half of August, the press, radio, and television hail the coming event. There are numerous speeches, human interest stories, interviews with famous persons, etc., all emphasizing the importance of education, paying tribute to teachers, dilating upon the values and joys of school experience, and congratulating the young upon their entry into a "new, wonderful phase" of their lives. When the day arrives, the children proceed to school, accompanied by their parents, brothers, sisters, and friends of the family. Everyone carries flowers. In front of the school doors, there is a ceremony with short speeches by the school director, the president of the parents' organization, leading citizens, and (as I once learned to my dismay) so-called distinguished visitors. After the speeches, a hand bell is rung by one of the first-graders (in this case, the smallest of the lot), and the youngsters enter the building to present bouquets to their teachers.

The gesture is not without general significance, for it reflects the generally positive attitude of children, and indeed the entire society, toward teachers of the young. This positive orientation is maintained throughout the school years. The teacher is generally regarded and treated as a friend. Outside of school hours, it is not uncommon to see a teacher surrounded by gaily chatting pupils, attending a play, a concert, the circus, or simply out for a walk. Nor is the enterprise a class project, but

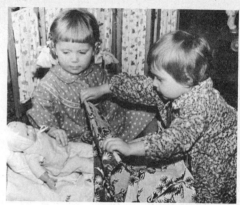

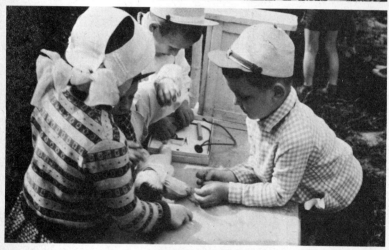

Role-playing is regarded
as an important part of
the socialization process.

"Kacca" means "cashier."

A trip to the beach is part of the kindergarten experience in the Krasnodarsk region.

The children take on further responsibilities as they grow.

rather a social occasion. Although there are, of course, exceptions, in general the relationship of children to teachers in the U.S.S.R. is perhaps best characterized as one of affectionate respect.

GOALS: GENERAL AND SPECIFIC

Probably the most important difference between Soviet and American schools is the emphasis placed in the former not only on subject matter, but equally on *vospitanie*, a term for which there is no exact equivalent in English; it might best be translated as "upbringing" or "character education." *Vospitanie* has as its stated aim the development of "Communist morality." The nature of Communist morality, its component traits, and the specific techniques for developing these traits in children are elaborated in great detail in an extensive literature including official manuals, books by leading authorities like V. A. Sukhomlinsky,[3] and innumerable articles in the popular press and in magazines totally devoted to the subject (e.g., *Vospitanie, Semya i shkola*). As with discussions of family upbringing, there is a large area of common ground in all these writings. We may take as a definitive example the official manual prepared by the Academy of Pedagogical Sciences entitled *The Program of the Upbringing Work of the School*.[4] This volume sets forth the "model program of upbringing" to be employed in all schools, whether traditional or of the "new type" (boarding and extended-day schools).* Objectives are stated in the form of general traits and modes of behavior to be developed in the child. These are organized under five major headings with some variation by age as reflected in Table 1, which illustrates goals outlined for the youngest (seven to eleven years) and oldest (sixteen to eighteen years) groups.

Although each trait is discussed in considerable detail in the text, the most revealing information regarding the content of character education in Soviet schools is provided by the specific

---

* Schools of the new type are expected to give even greater emphasis than the regular day schools to the development of Communist morality.

activities recommended for developing the desired characteristics. For each grade level, there are separate sections on behavior at school, in the home, and in the community. Below are some examples of activities prescribed in connection with the first three objectives (Communist morality, learning, and cul-

Gardening is another communal responsibility.

The children are clearing snow from the grounds of "our kindergarten."

tured conduct). To illustrate the progression with age, material is presented from two grade levels: Grade I (age seven) and Grade V (age twelve). The latter was chosen because it is the grade level at which we conducted systematic research and, therefore, we can provide some independent information about the results of training (*see below, pages 76–81*).

GRADE I

In school. All pupils are to arrive at school and in the classroom on time, wipe their feet upon entering, greet the teacher and all technical staff by name, give a general greeting to classmates and personal greeting by name to one's seatmate, keep one's things in order, obey all instructions of the teacher, learn rules of class conduct (standing when spoken to, proper position in listening, reading, and writing), learn and fulfill special classroom duties such as those of monitor, sanitarian, class librarian, teacher's assistent, gardener, etc. [For example, see duties of class monitor illustrated on pages 32–33.]

Youngsters give every appearance of flourishing under their "regime."

At home. Upon rising, greet one's parents, thank them after the meal or for any help received; before leaving, check to make sure you have everything necessary; upon return from school put everything in its place; take care of your own things (e.g., sew on buttons, iron, shine shoes, keep desk in order); in accordance with ability, help with house-cleaning, dusting, setting table and chairs in place, serving, clearing, washing dishes, growing and caring for decorative flowers, taking care of younger children—playing games with them and taking them for walks; do homework; follow the rule: "Job done—take a rest, then start another job."

In public places. Behave calmly; obey all requests of elders; do not disturb others by loud noise or running; yield right of way to grown-ups; don't litter; dissuade friends in time from engaging in bad behavior; acquaint yourself with public transportation and stops in your district; explore neighboring streets, squares, parks, scenic places; visit local workshops, sovkhozes, kolkhozes, garages, etc., and

A classroom collective plans a weekend camping trip to the outskirts of Moscow.

TABLE 1[a]

Summary of Stated Objectives of Upbringing for Youngest (7–11) and Oldest (16–18) Age Groups

AGES 7–11	AGES 16–18
Communist morality	
Sense of good and bad behavior	Collectivism, duty, honor, and conscience
Truthfulness, honesty, kindness	Development of will, patience, perseverance
Atheism: science *vs.* superstition	
Self-discipline	
Diligence in work and care of possessions	A Communist attitude toward work and public property
Friendship with classmates	Socialist humanism
Love of one's own locality and the Motherland	Soviet patriotism and proletarian internationalism
Responsible attitude toward learning	
Interest and striving for knowledge and skill	Understanding of the social significance of education
Industry in study	Perseverance and initiative in learning
Organizing intellectual and physical work	Increasing one's power of intellectual work (learning to plan one's work better, development of good work habits, self-criticism, etc.)
Striving to apply one's knowledge and ability in life and work	

AGES 7–11	AGES 16–18
	Cultured conduct
Care, accuracy, and neatness	Assimilation of norms of socialist community life
Courtesy and cordiality	Good manners and standards of behavior
Proper behavior on the street and in public places	
Cultured speech	
	Bases of esthetic culture
Understanding of the beautiful in nature, in the conduct of people, and in creative art	Esthetic appreciation of nature, social life, and works of art
Artistic creativity	Artistic creativity
	Physical culture and sport
Concern for strengthening and conditioning one's body	Maximizing the development of physical skills
Sanitary-hygienic habits	Mastering the rules of personal and social hygiene and sanitation
Preparation for sport and athletics	Training and participation in sports
	Mastering hiking and camping skills

[a] Adapted from N. I. Boldyrev (ed.), *Programma vospitatelnoi raboty shkoly* [*The Program of the Upbringing Work of the School*] (Moscow: Izdatelstvo Akademii Pedagogicheskikh Nauk RSFSR, 1960), 20–25, 110–118.

"Arrive at school well before lessons begin."

"Prepare chalk and erasing rag."

"During recess see that all children go outdoors."

"Ventilate the classroom."

"After the lesson, check neatness of desks."

"Dust furniture."

THE DUTIES OF THE CLASS MONITOR

"Water the flowers."

"Prepare any needed visual aids."

"Clean the blackboards."

"Prepare all materials necessary
for the next lesson."

"Polish the floor."

"Submit report and present the
classroom to the school monitor."

THE DUTIES OF THE CLASS MONITOR

become acquainted with how people work there for the common good; learn about the work the grown-ups in your family do for the service of the people.[5]

Activities to be carried on outside of school are frequently described in class, sometimes by posters like those shown on the facing page, rehearsed through role playing, and systematically reported on in school. In addition, there are equally detailed specifications for activities related to the two remaining goal areas: "strengthening health and physical prowess" and "developing creative capacities." We turn next to examples of specific activities recommended for fifth grade children.

GRADE V

In school. Perform all schoolwork carefully; work in an organized fashion; assist the teacher in setting up visual aids and uncomplicated instructional materials: keep a daily notebook of all work and submit it regularly for examination and signature by parents; during free hours assist classmates with their academic work; participate in getting fuel for heating the school (chopping wood), cleaning up and repairing school property and equipment, removing snow; act as a monitor in the dining hall; plan and make decorations for the classroom; care for the school garden and for trees and shrubs on the school grounds; supervise brigades of school children in cleaning up school property; supervise activities with primary classes (conducting games, taking them for walks, preparing gifts for them); participate in uncomplicated repair of school buildings; and assist younger classes in developing habits of good conduct toward their parents and elders, respect for their friends, showing concern for their sick friends, giving help according to one's abilities, fulfilling rules of conduct in home, school, and on the street, proper posture in sitting in class and standing to talk with grown-ups, obeying traffic regulations, etc.

At home. Help with home chores and cooking meals (breakfast, dinner, and supper); assist parents in the home gar-

"Take care of your clothes and footwear."

"Keep your room in order."

"Help your parents."

"AT HOME YOU ARE A HELPER"

den; cultivate your own garden beds, plant berry bushes and fruit trees, care for them and carry out observations on them; help eliminate agricultural pests; help maintain the courtyard, keeping it clear of snow; help care for elderly members of the family and younger children, teaching the latter how to take care of themselves; follow rules of accident prevention; organize your own study corner; fulfill all school assignments; start a home library, systematically repair schoolbooks; etc.

Other civic activities. Assist in children's nurseries and kindergartens; help conduct drives for scrap metal, paper, etc.; collect medicinal plants; participate in planting of fruit trees and decorative plants along roads, ravines, and public places; obey rules of street traffic; show cultured behavior in public places, etc.[6]

It is to be understood that all of the above activities, including those carried out at home, are conducted in the context of the child's collective. Specifically, each classroom is a unit of the Communist youth organization appropriate to that age level: the Octobrists for the first three grades (ages seven to nine), the Pioneers in grades IV–VIII (ages ten to fifteen), and the Komsomol [Young Communist League] in the higher grades and beyond to the age of twenty-eight. Membership in the Octobrists and Pioneers is virtually universal. The Komsomol, which is selective, enrolls over half of those eligible by age, with the proportion being considerably higher among young people still in school.[7]

The aims and values of these organizations, particularly at the school age level, are of a piece with those promulgated for the school program itself. This is readily apparent from the codes of the Octobrists and the Pioneers, which every child must learn; the rules of the Octobrists are listed in Table 2, and the Laws of the Pioneers are illustrated by the posters on pages 39–48. Some readers may be impressed by the similarity between these Communist precepts for the young and those promulgated by Western youth organizations like the Boy Scouts.

TABLE 2

Rules of the Octobrists[a]

1. Octobrists are future Pioneers.
2. Octobrists are diligent, study well, like school, and respect grown-ups.
3. Only those who like work are called Octobrists.
4. Octobrists are honest and truthful children.
5. Octobrists are good friends, read, draw, live happily.

[a] I. A. Kirov (ed.), *Pedagogicheskii slovar* [*Pedagogical Dictionary*], 2 vols, (Moscow: Izdatelstvo Akademii Pedagogicheskikh Nauk, 1960), II, 38.

For example, the slogan on the emblem *"Vsegda gotov"* means "Always prepared." There are some possible differences, however, in interpretation. One of these is reflected in the poster on page 45 illustrating the seventh law: "A Pioneer tells the truth and treasures the honor of his unit." As the drawing indicates, being truthful includes, as one Soviet educator preferred to put it, "expressing one's opinion publicly about a comrade's misconduct." (Note that the shamed seatmate had carved his name on the desk.) But there is a poster within the poster. It depicts a serious-faced Pioneer named Pavlik Morozov. Although the name is unfamiliar to most Westerners, it is a household word in the U.S.S.R. A young Pioneer during the period of collectivization, Pavlik denounced his own father as a collaborator with the Kulaks and testified against him in court. Pavlik was killed by people of the village for revenge, and is now regarded as a martyr in the cause of communism. A statue of him in Moscow is constantly visited by children, who keep it bedecked with fresh flowers, and many collective farms, Pioneer palaces, and libraries bear his name.

METHODS OF COLLECTIVE UPBRINGING

As already indicated, the organization of the youth groups parallels that of the school. The classes, designated as detachments, together comprise the overall school organization known as a *druzhina*. In addition, each classroom is further subdivided into *zvenya* [links], which typically correspond to the rows of double-seated school desks. It is this series of "nested" social units that constitutes the successive collectives of which each child is a member, and which carries primary responsibility for guiding his behavior and character development.

As indicated in the Introduction, the principles and methods employed are those developed by A. S. Makarenko. In the early nineteen-twenties, as a young school teacher and devout Communist, Makarenko was handed the assignment of setting up a rehabilitation program for some of the hundreds of homeless children who were roaming the Soviet Union after the civil wars. The first group of such children assigned to Makarenko's school, a ramshackle building far out of town, turned out to be a group of boys about eighteen years of age with extensive court records of housebreaking, armed robbery, and manslaughter. For the first few months, Makarenko's school served simply as the headquarters for the band of highwaymen who were his legal wards. But gradually, through the development of his group-oriented discipline techniques, and through what can only be called the compelling power of his own moral convictions, Makarenko was able to develop a sense of group responsibility and commitment to the work program and code of conduct that he had laid out for the collective. In the end, his Gorky Colony became known throughout the Soviet Union for its high morale, for its discipline, and for the productivity of its fields, farms, and shops. Indeed, Makarenko's methods proved so successful that he was selected to head a new commune set up by the Ministry of Internal Affairs (then the Cheka, later to become the GPU and NKVD). Makarenko described his experiences, theories, and methods in an extensive series of semi-autobiographical novels and essays which take up seven volumes in the edition of 1957. His works are widely read not only in the Soviet Union, but throughout the Communist world. In the West, his principal writings have been published in all major countries, with the notable exception of the United States, where a first translation did not appear until 1967 under the editorship of the present author.[8] English editions of his most important works have been published in Moscow, but are not readily available in the United States.

ПИОНЕР ЧТИТ ПАМЯТЬ ТЕХ, КТО ОТДАЛ СВОЮ ЖИЗНЬ В БОРЬБЕ ЗА СВОБОДУ И ПРОЦВЕТАНИЕ СОВЕТСКОЙ РОДИНЫ.

1. A pioneer honors the memory of those who have given their life in the struggle for freedom and the flowering of the Soviet Motherland.

2. A Pioneer is a friend to children of all the nations of the world.

ПИОНЕР ПРИЛЕЖНО УЧИТСЯ, ДИСЦИПЛИНИРОВАН И ВЕЖЛИВ.

3. A Pioneer studies diligently, is disciplined, and courteous.

Пионер любит
трудиться
и бережет
народное добро.

4. A Pioneer likes to work and takes good care of public property.

Пионер—хороший товарищ, заботится о младших, помогает старшим.

5. A Pioneer is a good friend, cares for younger children, and helps grown-ups.

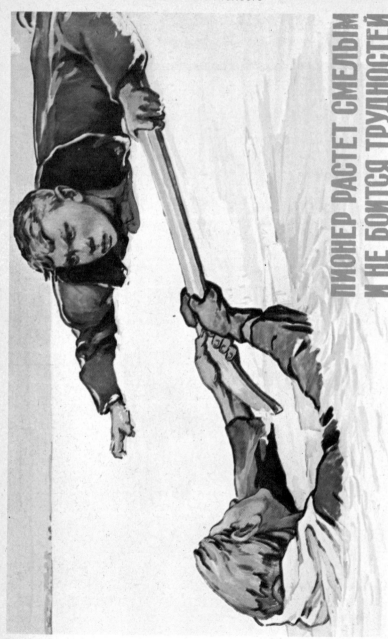

ПИОНЕР РАСТЕТ СМЕЛЫМ
И НЕ БОИТСЯ ТРУДНОСТЕЙ

6. A Pioneer develops courage and does not fear difficulties.

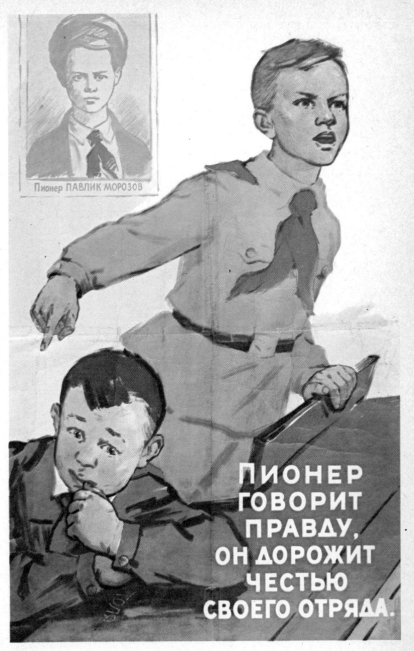

Пионер ПАВЛИК МОРОЗОВ

ПИОНЕР
ГОВОРИТ
ПРАВДУ,
ОН ДОРОЖИТ
ЧЕСТЬЮ
СВОЕГО ОТРЯДА.

7. A Pioneer tells the truth and treasures the honor of his unit.

Пионер закаляет себя, каждый день делает физкультурную зарядку.

8. A Pioneer develops his physique, does physical exercises every day.

Пионер любит природу, он защитник зеленых насаждений, полезных птиц, и животных.

9. A Pioneer loves nature; he is a protector of green plants, useful birds and animals.

ПИОНЕР-ВСЕМ РЕБЯТАМ ПРИМЕР!

10. A Pioneer is an example to all children.

Makarenko's influence extends far beyond his voluminous writings, since there is scarcely a manual for the guidance of Communist parents, teachers, or youth workers that does not draw heavily on his theories and techniques, which now constitute the central core of Soviet educational practice. As carried out in Soviet schools, his approach places major emphasis on work, group competitiveness, and collective discipline. Work takes the form of class projects such as gardening and community service, as well as specific training in skills like carpentry, metal work, automotive mechanics, dressmaking, radio repair, computer programming, and the building of scale models for science and industry.

An equally prominent role is played by "socialist competition" between successive levels of collectives, first between the individual "links," then between classes, schools, and finally cities and regions. This competition involves all phases of activity and behavior: sports, shop work, service projects, housekeeping, personal grooming, moral conduct, etc. The over-

Gardening is a class project included in "socialist competition."

all status of each pupil is evaluated weekly by his peers, following standards and procedures taught by the upbringers. Since each child's status depends in part on the standing of the collective of which he is a member, it is to each pupil's enlightened self-interest to watch over his neighbor, encourage the other's good performance and behavior, and help him when he is in difficulty. In this system the children's collective becomes the agent of adult society and the major source of reward and punishment. The latter typically takes the form of group sanctions expressed through public criticism and, ultimately, the threat of exclusion from membership. The individual is taught to set the judgment of the group above his own and to subordinate his interests to those of the collective.

An especially prominent feature of collective upbringing is the emphasis on altruistic behavior both at the individual and social level. Not only are the members of the collective taught to help each other, but, through the system of *shevstvo*, perhaps best described as "group adoption," each class takes on responsibility for the upbringing of a group of children at a lower

The Soviet child is trained in vocational skills.

grade level. For example, a fourth grade class "adopts" a first grade class in the same school; the older children escort the younger ones to school, play with them in the school yard, teach them new games, read to them, help them with schoolwork—in general, act as older brothers and sisters. Moreover the manner in which they fulfill this civic responsibility enters into the evaluation of their total school performance as a regular part of school activities. Finally, the system of "adoption" embraces adult collectives in the outside world so that each school may also be a "ward" of a shop in a factory, or of a bureau of a municipal agency, with the workers devoting their spare time to activities with or in behalf of "our class" at the neighborhood school. Such arrangements reflect the far wider involvement of adult organizations in the lives of children than is common in our own country.

We see, then, that at all levels, from the row within the classroom to the farm or factory outside the school, the collective stands at the heart of the process of *vospitanie*. In Makarenko's words, ironically expressed in a familiar cadence, the child is to be brought up "in the collective, by the collective, and for the collective."

COLLECTIVE UPBRINGING IN ACTION

What does it mean concretely to be brought up "in the collective, by the collective, and for the collective"? For an answer, we turn again to our two major sources on the translation of theory into practice: Soviet instructional manuals and our own field observations.

For an example from the former, we draw on a small volume by L. I. Novikova,[9] prepared by staff members of the Institute on the Theory and History of Pedagogy at the Academy of Pedagogical Sciences for the training and guidance of "school directors, supervisors, teachers, and Pioneer leaders." The manual is typical of a number of books published on the same subject during recent years.[10] Like the other manuals, the one by Novikova contains numerous examples of procedures and events observed in actual classrooms.

Girls as well as boys are given instruction in metal-working.

The book is entitled *Socialist Competition in the Schools,* and the same theme is echoed in the titles of the individual chapters, "Competition in the Classroom," "Competition between Classrooms," "Competition between Schools," and so on. We see here reflected the influence of a well-known principle of dialectical materialism: Conflict at one level is resolved through synthesis at the next higher level.

Let us examine the process of collective socialization as it is initiated in the very first grade. Conveniently enough, the manual starts us off on the first day of school with the teacher standing before the newly assembled class. What should her first words be? Our text tells us:

> It is not difficult to see that a direct approach to the class with the command, "All sit straight," often doesn't bring the desired effect since a demand in this form does not reach the sensibilities of the pupils and does not activate them.[11]

How does one "reach the sensibilities of the pupils" and "activate them"? According to the manual, here is what the teacher

The students are shown how to operate a movie projector.

This is an automotive mechanics shop.

Girls have the opportunity to learn dressmaking.

should say: "Let's see which row can sit the straightest."[12] This approach, we are told, has certain important psychological advantages. In response:

> The children not only try to do everything as well as possible themselves, but also take an evaluative attitude toward those who are undermining the achievement of the row. If similar measures arousing the spirit of competition in the children are systematically applied by experienced teachers in the primary classes, then gradually the children themselves begin to monitor the behavior of their comrades and remind those of them who forget about the rules set by the teacher, not to forget what needs to be done and what should not be done. The teacher soon has helpers.[13]

The manual then goes on to describe how records are kept for each row from day to day for different types of tasks so that the young children can develop a concept of group excellence over time and over a variety of activities, including personal cleanliness, condition of notebooks, conduct in passing from one room to the other, quality of recitations in each subject matter, and so on. In these activities considerable emphasis is placed on the externals of behavior in dress, manner, and speech. There must be no spots on shirt or collar, shoes must be shined, pupils must never pass a teacher without stopping to greet him, there must be no talking without permission, and the like. Charts are displayed in the schools showing the performance of each row in every type of activity, together with their total overall standing. "Who is Best?" the charts ask, but the entries are not by individuals but by social units—rows, and later the "cells" of the Octobrists, the Communist youth organization which reaches down to the primary grades.

At first it is the teacher who sets the standards. But soon, still in the first grade, a new wrinkle is introduced: responsible monitors are designated in each row for each activity. In the beginning their job is only to keep track of the merits and demerits assigned each row by the teacher. Different children act as monitors for different activities and, according to the manual, become very involved in the progress of their row. Then

In what way is the doll's corner shown in the book better than Masha's?

Why will Aunt Kate be angry with Vova but praise Lenochka?

Why is Fedya considered a good brother?

too, group achievement is not without its rewards. The winning row is allowed to leave first when class is dismissed. One of the highest rewards for a Pioneer unit is to be photographed "in parade uniforms," and this photograph is published in that pervasive Soviet institution, the wall newspaper. (Soviet children are supposed to wear school uniforms—in practice, only the blouse or red kerchief may be in evidence. Uniforms are expensive.) The significance of achievements is still further enhanced by the introduction of competition among classes so that the winning class and the winning "link" are visited by delegates from other classrooms in recognition of their excellent performance.

Now let us look more closely at this teacher-mediated monitoring process. In the beginning, we are told, the first grade teacher attempts to focus the attention of children on the achievements of the group; that is, she accentuates the positive. But, gradually, "It becomes necessary to take account of negative facts which interfere with the activity of the class."[14] As an example we are given the instance of a child who, despite warnings, continues to arrive in class a few minutes after the bell has rung. The teacher decides that the time has come to invoke the group process in correcting such behavior. Accordingly, the next time that Serezha is late, she stops him at the door and turns to the class with this question: "Children, is it helpful or not helpful to us to have Serezha come in late?" The answers are quick in coming. "It interferes." "He ought to come on time." "Well," says the teacher, "How can we help Serezha with this problem?"[15] There are many suggestions: get together to buy him a watch, exile him from the classroom, send him to the director's office, or even to exile him from the school. But apparently these proposals are either not appropriate or too extreme. The teacher, our text tells us, "helps the children find the right answer." She asks for a volunteer to stop by and pick Serezha up on the way to school. Many children offer to help in this mission.

But tragedy stalks. The next day it turns out that not only is Serezha late, but also the boy who had promised to pick him up.

Since they are both from the same link, their unit receives two sets of demerits and falls to lowest place. Group members are keenly disappointed. "Serezha especially suffered much and felt himself responsible, but equal blame was felt by his companion who had forgotten to stop in for him."[16]

In this way, both through concrete action and explanation, the teacher seeks to forge a spirit of group unity and responsibility. From time to time, she explains to the children the significance of what they are doing:

> They have to learn to live together as one friendly family, since they will have to be learning together for all of the next ten years, and for this reason one must learn how to help one's companions and to treat them decently.[17]

By the time the children are in the second grade, the responsibilities expected of them are increased in complexity. For example, instead of simply recording the evaluations made by the teacher, the monitors are taught how to make the evaluations themselves. Since this is rather difficult, in the beginning two

In the Pioneers' council room, members prepare
to deliberate Ivanov's case.

monitors are assigned to every task. In this way, our text tells us, they can help each other in doing a good job of evaluation.

Here is a third grade classroom:

Class 3-B is just an ordinary class; it's not especially well-disciplined nor is it outstandingly industrious. It has its lazy members and its responsible ones, quiet ones and active ones, daring, shy, and immodest ones.

The teacher has led this class now for three years, and she has earned the affection, respect, and acceptance as an authority from her pupils.* Her word is law for them.

The bell has rung, but the teacher has not yet arrived. She has delayed deliberately in order to check on how the class will conduct itself.

In the class all is quiet. After the noisy class break, it isn't so easy to mobilize yourself and to quell the restlessness within you! Two monitors at the desk silently observe

* Note that this practice differs from that followed in American schools where elementary teachers instruct a new group of children each year.

The Council proposed and debated various forms and degrees of punishment for the boys who went swimming without supervision.

the class. On their faces is reflected the full importance and seriousness of the job they are performing. But there is no need for them to make any reprimands: the youngsters with pleasure and pride maintain scrupulous discipline; they are proud of the fact that their class conducts itself in a manner that merits the confidence of the teacher. And when the teacher enters and quietly says to be seated, all understand that she deliberately refrains from praising them for the quiet and order, since in their class it could not be otherwise. . . .

During the lesson, the teacher gives an exceptional amount of attention to collective competition between "links." Throughout the entire lesson the youngsters are constantly hearing which link has best prepared its lesson, which link has done the best at numbers, which is the most disciplined, which has turned in the best work.

The best link not only gets a verbal positive evaluation but receives the right to leave the classroom first during the break and to have its notebooks checked before the others. As a result, the links receive the benefit of collective education, common responsibility, and mutual aid.

"What are you fooling around for? You're holding up the whole link," whispers Kolya to his neighbor during the preparation period for the lesson. And during the break he teaches her how to organize better the books and pads in her knapsack.

"Work more carefully," says Olya to her girl friend. "See, on account of you, our link got behind today. You come to me and we'll work together at home."[18]

In the third grade still another innovation is introduced. The monitors are taught not only to evaluate but to state their criticisms publicly.

Here is a typical picture. It is the beginning of the lesson. In the first row the link leader reports, basing his comments on information submitted by the sanitarian and other responsible monitors: "Today Valodya did the wrong problem. Masha didn't write neatly and forgot to underline the right words in her lesson; Alyosha had a dirty shirt collar."

The other link leaders make similar reports [the Pioneers are sitting by rows].

The youngsters are not offended by this procedure: they understand that the link leaders are not merely tattle-telling, but simply fulfilling their duty. It doesn't even occur to the monitors and sanitarians to conceal the shortcomings of their comrades. They feel that they are doing their job well precisely when they notice one or another defect.[19]

Also in the third grade, the teacher introduces still another procedure. She now proposes that the children enter into competition with the monitors, and see if they can beat the monitor at his own game by criticizing themselves.

The results were spectacular: if the monitor was able to talk only about four or five members of the row, there would be supplementary reports about their own shortcomings from as many as eight or ten pupils.[20]

Nor does the process of social criticism and control stop with school. Our manual tells us that parents are asked to submit periodic reports to the school collective on the behavior of the child at home. One may wonder how parents can be depended on to turn in truthful accounts. And there is the large issue of the extent to which the picture painted by the professional protagonists of collective discipline corresponds with what another observer might see.

Some light is shed on these issues by the following excerpts from our field observations. The first presents a comparative view of American and Soviet discipline as revealed in an informal conversation with three Soviet school teachers. The second extract, recorded in a nursery, illustrates the process through which techniques of collective discipline are developed in the very young. The third, noted in a first grade classroom, shows how sanctions are applied in a fashion which provides for continuity of influence from the family and the peer collective. The fourth example, at the fifth grade level, shows a "forged, self-reliant" class collective in action. The final report, describing a meeting of a Pioneer soviet (i.e., student council), reveals the process of collective discipline operating at its highest level, that of the *druzhina,* or entire school.

"How do you keep discipline?"

I came into the crowded public dining room and sat down at a table with one empty seat. I was in luck. My three companions turned out to be elementary school teachers. They were curious about discipline techniques used in American schools. After I had given several examples, I was interrupted, "But how do you use the collective?" When I replied that we really did not use the classroom group in any systematic way, my three companions were puzzled. "But how do you keep discipline?"

Now it was my turn to ask for examples. "All right," came the answer, "Let us suppose that ten-year-old Vanya is pulling Anya's curls. If he doesn't stop the first time I speak to him, all I need do is mention it again in the group's presence; then I can be reasonably sure that before the class meets again the boy will be talked to by the officers of his Pioneer link. They will remind him that his behavior reflects on the reputation of the link."

"And what if he persists?"

"Then he may have to appear before his link—or even the entire collective—who will explain his misbehavior to him and determine his punishment."

"What punishment?"

"Various measures. He may just be censured, or if his conduct is regarded as serious, he may be expelled from membership. Very often he himself will acknowledge his faults before the group."

A Soviet TAT

In a secluded corner of the room, a group of about a dozen three-year-olds was clustered about an upbringer who was showing them a picture book.[21] On turning to each new page, the upbringer would ask, "Children, who can tell me a story about this picture?" A kind of TAT Soviet style.* But with an important difference. The Amer-

---

* The Thematic Apperception Test, a technique devised by the American psychologist Henry A. Murray for analyzing personality dynamics from stories told by the subject in response to a series of pictures.

ican TAT test has no right answers. Not so for its Soviet counterpart. Each of the pictures depicted a child engaged in some clearly desirable, or undesirable activity. On one page, a little girl was shown reading a picture book depicting a neat room, while her own room is messy and cluttered (*see top of page* 56); in another, a boy tracks into the house with muddy feet, while his sister is carefully wiping hers on the mat (*see middle of page* 56).

But telling stories was only part of it. As I watched, the upbringer showed the picture of a little boy buttoning a heavy overcoat for his younger sister (*see bottom of page* 56). After obtaining a correct explanation of the scene from an eager lad in a bright red suit, the upbringer pointed to the picture and asked, "We have helpful children here, too, but do we have anyone in our collective who doesn't help?"

The children looked about. One after another fixed their eyes on a pretty little girl in blue. "Masha," they said. "She doesn't help." Masha looked up wide-eyed and then lowered her head, almost weeping.

But the upbringer came to her rescue. "Masha used to do things like that, but doesn't any longer. We all see her helping gladly now."

Larissa Forgets

The calendar in this first grade classroom reads April 3. It is a lovely spring morning. A vase of pussywillows stands in the window. One by one the children are asked to come to the front of the room to recite a poem each was to have memorized for today. It tells about the melting snow, the birds, the furry willow buds. About a third of the youngsters have taken their turn, each declaiming the four or five stanzas in that special emotionally elevated tone that Russians employ in reciting poetry. So far, there has not been a single lapse in memory.

It is now Larissa's turn. She walks primly to the front of the room, starts off bravely and finishes two stanzas. Suddenly, silence. Larissa has forgotten. There is no prompting, either from teacher or from friends. The silence continues.

Then the teacher speaks, softly but firmly, "Larissa, you have disappointed your mother, you have disappointed your father, and above all, you have disappointed your comrades who are sitting here before you. Go back to your place. They do not wish to hear anything more from you today."

With head down, Larissa silently returns to her seat, a teardrop flowing down each cheek.

Vova Neglects His Math

It was Friday noon and the five elected officers of the *soviet* [council] of Class 5–B were having their weekly meeting to evaluate each pupil. Normally no adult was present. The procedure required rating each class member on a scale of 1 to 5 on the basis of all aspects of his behavior: school grades (supplied by the teacher), cleanliness, execution of civic responsibilities, athletics, etc. The final mark was written on a slip of paper to be given to each child, who in turn had to take it home and have it acknowledged by a parent's signature.

The young people took their responsibilities very seriously. They were discussing Sasha, editor of the class newspaper. Lyolya, the class "commander" asked for a judgment. One of the youngsters offered the opinion that while the recent issues were good, there had been little originality, no new feature articles. "Well, then, let's give him a 4 instead of a 5," proposed another. "It may jack him up a bit."

The next case was more difficult. A month ago, Vova had been warned that he was doing poorly in arithmetic and pulling down his link. There had been no improvement.

After some discussion, Lyolya proposed: "I think this problem is serious enough to require action by the entire collective. We can call a special meeting for this afternoon."

At the class meeting, Vova, a handsome lad in a white shirt, is called forward and asked what he did yesterday upon returning home from school.

"As always, I cleaned house so that Mother wouldn't

have to do it when she got home. Then I did my home-work."

"What subjects?"

"English, history, some drawings for shop."

As no mention is made of math, the class officers exchange significant looks. In a stern voice, Chairman Lyolya reminds him: "A month ago, you were warned to work harder on your math, and now you don't even mention it."

Vova: "I didn't have any math homework that night."

Voice from the class: "You should have studied it anyway."

Lyolya asks the class for recommendations. After some discussion, a girl with a blue hair ribbon asks for the floor.

"I propose that we designate two of our classmates to supervise Vova as he does his math homework every night and give him help as needed."

Vova objects: "I don't need them. I can do it by myself. I promise."

But Lyolya is not impressed. Turning to Vova, she says quietly, "We have seen what you do by yourself. Now two of your classmates will work with you and when *they* say you are ready to work alone, we'll believe it."

Swimming Without Supervision

I was attending the weekly assembly of the Pioneer organization in a school-of-the-prolonged-day. After the presentation of the colors, the commander of each class reported to the entire student body his collective's achievements for the week. One group had planted flowers in a new housing project, another had built bookcases for a nearby nursery, and so on. After the recital, the Director of the school complimented the units on their accomplishments and then, turning to the assembled fifth-graders, addressed their bright-eyed, twelve-year-old commander, "Ivanov, on reporting on the achievements of your group, you omitted something. You failed to mention that only last evening you, the commander, and seven of your men went swimming without supervision. Such action reflects inadequacy not only in the class collective but in the entire Pioneer leadership and organization. I expect the Pioneers to deal appropriately with this matter."

After the meeting, I returned with the Director to his office. There awaiting us was a group of half a dozen adults. These were the parents of the offending boys. They had been summoned from their place of work at the Director's request. He received them in his office, one by one, as I sat by. His statement to each parent was almost the same. He spoke in a quiet, semi-formal tone, "You are called here because yesterday your son participated in unsupervised swimming. I expect that you will give him appropriate punishment."

With only one exception, the responses of the parents were equally uniform. "Thank you, Comrade Director; the punishment will be administered," each one said and promptly left the Director's office. One mother ventured an excuse, "I didn't know where he was." "Precisely," interrupted the Director. "That is exactly the problem. Nothing could be more serious. I would rather be told that your son is getting failing grades, or that he spoke rudely to a teacher. But when it is a matter of endangering his life, that must not be permitted."

But punishment by the parents was only an ancillary penalty. The main disciplinary action, I learned, would take place at four that afternoon when the *soviet druzhina*, or executive council, of the school Pioneer organization would deliberate over Ivanov's case.

Let us attend the meeting. We find ourselves in the council room, an impressive chamber lined with banners and trophies. Around the large table, covered with a deep-red cloth, sit the elected members of the Council (*see page 58*). There are thirteen of them, nine girls and four boys, representing all classes from the fifth grade upward.

Ironically, Ivanov, as commander in the fifth grade class, is a member of the group. After completing the routine totaling of class points for the weekly standings in interclass competition in behavioral excellence, the Council turns to its special business. Ivanov is asked to stand and tell the group what he has done. The answer is barely audible, "I went swimming."

As his answers are written down by the secretary, a girl

asks: "You and who else?"

He names seven others.

Second girl: "Fine thing, you the commander leading your men."

A boy: "Do you realize that last year a child drowned in that very pond?"

The questions and accusations continue, mostly from the girls. The major effort is two-sided: first, to impress Ivanov with the fact that, in violating the rule, he had jeopardized the lives of his classmates as well as his own; second, that his act constituted a betrayal of the faith invested in him as a Pioneer commander. Ivanov is now speechless. He trembles slightly and is struggling to hold back the tears. The direction of questions shifts: "Who suggested the idea of going swimming in the first place?" Silence. "Was it you?" Ivanov shakes his head. "Then who was it?" No answer.

One of the older girls speaks up. She is a ninth-grader and already a *Komsomolka*, or member of the Young Communist League. "All right, Ivanov, if you won't tell us, how would you like it if your whole class doesn't get to go on our five-day camporee next week?"

Another girl: "You will all just stay here and work."

Still another: "Think how the rest of your classmates will feel about you then."

Third girl: "Why punish the rest of the class? They didn't have anything to do with it."

Someone suggests punishing just the boys. Now the male council members, who have said very little, raise an objection. The full collective is responsible for the conduct of its members, they say. Besides, they argue, punishing only the boys would set up a division between the sexes, and that is against Communist principles!

Other measures are proffered. Someone suggests that the boys be restricted from swimming for the rest of the summer. Others feel that they should be disqualified from participation in summer camp. There is a proposal that they be given special chores to do during the vacation, such as watering trees. During this discussion, the adult leader of the Pioneers, who had come in some time after the session had started and had been listening attentively on the sidelines, asks for the floor. He suggests that it makes no sense to impose a punishment for the rest of the summer, since the offense itself will be forgotten and only the punishment remembered. As for finding the instigator, the rest of the offenders should be required to speak for themselves. "Let's call in the rest of them."

Seven boys file in. The previous procedure is repeated. Each one is asked if he participated in the swimming and each admits it. Then each is asked if he initiated the enterprise. All either deny it or refuse to answer. Again the Council members explain the seriousness of the offense and discuss possible punishments. Again there is talk of forbidding the boys to attend the five-day camporee, the school's major spring outing. Mention is also made of special work assignments. And one new idea is introduced. A girl member proposes that until further notice the boys be deprived of the privilege of wearing their Pioneer kerchiefs. The boys are having a hard time facing their accusers. Some bow their heads; others give in at the knees.

Again it is the adult leader who eases the pressure. Although his voice is stern, the effect of his remarks is to set aside one of the severe suggestions: "This is certainly a serious matter. I would recommend that all eight of the offenders be placed on strict probation for the coming week, and if any one of them deviates so much as a jot or a tittle from the code of proper conduct, he will be deprived of the privilege of attending the camporee."

The Council accepts the suggestion but in its final decision adds two further penalties. All the boys look up as sentence is passed in solemn instruction by Nadya, the Council President: "Ivanov, first of all, it is your responsibility to see to it that beginning on Monday, neither you nor any of your men are to wear your Pioneer kerchiefs." The President continues, "Second, during the coming week, while you are on probation, each of you is to carry out an extra work assignment by watering all the newly planted trees on the school grounds every day. Finally, before you go home this evening, all of you can scrub down and wax the floor in the school assembly."

When I left the school at 6:15, the last part of the sentence was being carried out, as the boys worked their way across the wide floor of the auditorium.

The foregoing examples would seem to indicate that Soviet methods of collective upbringing rely primarily on negative criticism. This is not the case. Incidents of the type recorded above do not occur very often. For example, I looked through the minutes of the Pioneer Council which had tried Ivanov and his comrades. The last trial had occurred more than a year before; the culprits were two teenagers caught drinking a bottle of wine. In general the prevailing atmosphere in Soviet classrooms and other children's collectives is one of acceptance and approval for the work being done. The carrot is much more in evidence than the stick. What is distinctive, however, is the saliency of the collective as the focus of reward. For example, the great charts emblazoned "Who is Best?", which bedeck the halls and walls of schools and classrooms, have as entries the names not of individual pupils but of rows and links. It is the winning unit that is rewarded with a pennant or a special privilege, or by having a picture taken. And when praise is given, as it frequently is, to an individual child, the group referent is usually there: "Today Pyotr helped Katya, and as a result his unit did not get behind the rest."

This, then, is the process of collective upbringing. For a Westerner, it may seem a far cry from the world of the family with its informal, personalized, and private expressions of parental affection and authority. Yet, for the Soviet child, there is considerable psychological continuity between the two contexts. Both are strong sources of security, support, and satisfaction; and in both deviance is interpreted as emotional betrayal and is responded to by withdrawal of acceptance and mobilization of guilt.

In the light of such continuity across the two major contexts of socialization for the Soviet child, what kind of outcomes can we expect in terms of personality development? It is to this challenging question that we now turn.

3

The Psychological Implications
of Soviet Methods of Upbringing

WE BEGIN our analysis by considering the possible impact on a child of the pattern of demonstrative maternal warmth to which Russian youngsters are exposed from earliest infancy. The most relevant research in this connection is found in the pioneering studies of Percival M. Symonds and David M. Levy,[1] along with more recent investigations summarized in reviews by Wesley C. Becker, Urie Bronfenbrenner, Bettye M. Caldwell, John A. Clausen, and Willard W. Hartup.[2] In general, these researches point to the conclusion that a warm, constricting mother-child relationship maximizes dependency and produces a child who is readily socialized to adult standards. One can hardly improve on the original description provided by Symonds' own concise summary of the syndrome as he found it in America of the nineteen-thirties. He characterized children growing up in such a context as "obedient, orderly, submissive," and likely to "conform to the modes of the group in which they are reared. . . . This is a fair picture of the good child in our society." "The only trouble," he went on to say, "is that the men in our society are supposed to be independent, aggressive, forward, self-confident and strong."[3]

The Effects of Affection and its Withdrawal

The later investigations were not only more sophisticated but made an important new contribution by identifying the disciplinary strategy involved in inducing conformity with adult standards. In summarizing these research findings, the present author described parents using this strategy in the following terms:

> . . . they reason with the youngster, isolate him, appeal to guilt, show disappointment—in short, convey in a variety of ways, on the one hand the kind of behavior that is expected of the child; on the other, the realization that transgression means the interruption of a mutually valued relationship. . . .
>
> The successful use of withdrawal of love as a disciplinary technique implies the prior existence of a gratifying relationship; the more love present in the first instance, the greater the threat implied in its withdrawal. . . . Our data indicate that it is primarily mothers who tend to employ "love oriented" techniques of discipline. . . .[4]

The foregoing analysis, derived from research done only with American children, would seem to apply rather well to patterns of child rearing in the Soviet family.

Father Absence and the Mother-Centered Family

The question may be raised as to how this particular pattern developed? How did it come about that the Soviet parents, especially mothers, are so affectionate with children and react to disobedience by withdrawal of love? Are these merely long-established cultural traits, passed down from one generation to the next, or are they promoted and maintained by certain social structural properties found in Russian society which, if they were altered, would modify the existing pattern?

Some light is shed on this issue by a growing body of research on the effects of father absence. Studies carried out both in the United States[5] and Norway[6] indicate that such absence not only affects the behavior of the child directly but also influences the mother in the direction of greater over-protectiveness. The effect of both of these tendencies is especially critical for boys. Children from father-absent homes, at least initially, are more submissive, dependent, effeminate, and susceptible to group influence, with the later course of development being determined by the character of the group in which the child finds himself. Thus in lower-class Negro families, where father absence is particularly common, the typically passive and dependent boy readily transfers his attachment to the gang, where, to earn and keep his place, he must demonstrate his toughness and aggressiveness.[7]

Similar but not so extreme effects are likely to occur in homes in which the father is present but plays a markedly subordinate role. In a study of the relation between parental role structure and the child's behavior, Bronfenbrenner[8] found that matriarchal families, in which primarily the mother held the power of decision, tended to produce children who "do not take initiative" and "look to others for direction and decision." At the same time, an asymmetrical family structure has somewhat different effects on the two sexes. Specifically:

> Both responsibility and leadership are fostered by the relatively greater salience of the parent of the same sex. . . . Boys tended to be more responsible when the father rather than the mother is the principal disciplinarian; girls are more dependable when the mother is the major authority figure.[9]

Further investigation qualified this finding in an important respect.[10] It revealed that children of both sexes showing the highest degrees of leadership and dependability tended to come neither from matriarchal nor patriarchal families, nor from those in which the mother and father participated equally and similarly in the process of child rearing; rather, such youngsters were found in families where both parents took an active part but behaved rather differently, with some division between supportive and disciplinary roles.

What is the relevance of all these considerations to child rearing in the U.S.S.R.? First of all, particularly during and after World War II, millions of Russian children were brought up in fatherless families, and, fifteen years after the war's end, there was still an excess of 20,000,000 women over men in the Soviet population.[11] Nor is this a new phenomenon in Russian history, which records an inexorable series of devastating invasions, civil wars, famines, massive exiles, and shifts in population, all of which had the effect of separating families and removing large numbers of men from their homes. Beyond the direct effect which such paternal absence would have had on the wives and children of missing fathers, there is the likelihood of an indirect impact of imposing matriarchal patterns in families where the father was physically present. Such an effect has been strongly indicated as one of the heritages of slavery in the Negro family of today,[12] and could well be operative in any society experiencing a history of massive, enforced family separation. In any event, despite the equalization of the sex ratio in the Soviet population over thirty-five years of age, which encompasses the present generation of parents of young children, the continuing primacy of the mother in child rearing is reflected both in objective circumstances (such as the common practice of the *kommandirovka*: a work assignment in another locality without being accompanied by one's family) and in the popular literature on family upbringing, in which the mother is portrayed and addressed not only as the chief agent of child rearing but also as the principal maker of decisions affecting the child. (Witness the instruction, on pages 13–14, for "silent treatment" of the disobedient child, in which a lengthy passage addressed to the mother ends, almost as an afterthought, with a reminder that "about the same behavior" should be shown by the father.)

Perhaps even more significant for the Soviet child is the fact that the saliency of females in his environment increases markedly upon his entry into nursery school, and continues thereafter. Even though some male teachers are to be found, especially at the secondary school level, the excess of female over male personnel is even more pronounced than in the United States. Moreover, the elected leaders of the peer collective are also likely to be girls (in the thirty or more schools, camps, and Pioneer palaces visited, there was only one instance in which the highest officer was a boy). Finally, as dramatically illustrated by the example of the trial, after the primary grades it is girls who take the most active role in collective discipline, and boys who are most likely to be its target.

Collective Upbringing in Social Psychological Perspective

These considerations bring us to our last and perhaps most difficult question: what are the psychological effects of collective upbringing? This question in turn may be examined from two points of view. First, what evidence do we have from Western research bearing on the consequences of child rearing in communal settings? Second, what is known about the characteristics of Soviet children who are products of this type of upbringing?

EVIDENCE FROM WESTERN RESEARCH

Since available data on the first of these questions has already been examined in some detail elsewhere,[13] we shall deal with the issue here only in summary form. Western studies relevant to the effects of collective upbringing derive principally from two major contexts. The first of these is, of course, the family. We have already seen that the practice of withdrawing group approval employed as a disciplinary measure in Soviet children's collectives has much in common with the "love-oriented" techniques, which research on American families has shown to be especially potent in effecting "good behavior" and making children "conform more closely to the modes of the group in which they are reared." This would suggest that analogous methods employed at a group level would have similar results. Moreover, the effectiveness of the collective in this regard would be enhanced by two distinctive features of the Soviet family already noted. The absence of a strong counterforce to the mother in the person of a frequently present and powerful father, coupled with the early diffusion of the nurturant role to persons outside the family should facilitate transition from the mother to the collective as a primary source of security and incontestable authority for the child.

A second body of research carrying implications for the effectiveness of collective upbringing deals with the power of the group in controlling the behavior of its members. Experiments on conformity behavior, notably the work on adult subjects by Solomon E. Asch, Morton Deutsch and Harold G. Gerard, and Stanley Milgram,[14] and on children by Ruth Berenda, M. S. Neimark, and Muzafer Sherif *et al.*,[15] testify to the power of the majority in shaping and regulating the behavior of group members and forcing the deviant individual to conform. Of particular significance for the Soviet case is Deutsch and Gerard's[16] ingenious extension of the classical work of Solomon Asch on group influences in perception.[17] In the original experiment as conducted by Asch, the subject, along with six or eight others, is asked to identify the longer of two straight lines presented for all to see. At first, the task seems simple enough. The lines are easy to discriminate; the subject hears others make their judgments and then makes his own. In the beginning he is in agreement, but gradually he notices that the judgments offered by others do not correspond with his own. Actually the experiment is rigged, the other group members having been instructed to give incorrect responses on a predetermined schedule. The effect on the subjects is disturbing enough so that in a third of the cases they follow the false lead of the majority. In designing their own experiment, Deutsch and Gerard took note of the fact that in the earlier work the subjects were not actually members of a "group"; they were simply a collection of strangers assembled in one room to participate in an experiment. If a prior sense of group consciousness had been developed before the perceptual task, they argued, the distorting influence of social pressure would have been more pronounced. They then proceeded to test this hypothesis by running two series of experiments. The first simply replicated Asch's original conditions; the second introduced before the perceptual task a procedure designed to enhance feelings of group membership. The results were strongly confirmatory: the subjects in the "group" condition made twice as many errors (i.e., distortions) as the controls run under the standard conditions.

What was the procedure used to develop a feeling of group identity? Immediately before being asked to make perceptual judgments, the experimental subjects were instructed as follows:

> This group is one of twenty similar groups who are participating in this experiment. We are going to give a reward to the five best groups—the five groups that make the fewest errors on the series of judgments that you are given. The reward will be a pair of tickets to a Broadway play of your own choosing for each member of the winning group. An error will be counted any time one of you makes an incorrect judgment. . . . The five groups that make the best scores will be rewarded.[18]

In short, as their experimental treatment designed to enhance the Asch effect, Deutsch and Gerard employed "socialist competition." The only modification a Soviet upbringer could wish would be to have the winning team make a group decision on which play to see and then attend the theater as a "victorious collective."

In summary, on the basis of Western research both on parent-child relations and on group process, one would expect Soviet methods of child rearing both in the family and in the children's collective to reinforce each other in producing a child who conforms to adult standards of "good conduct."

STUDIES OF SOVIET CHILDREN

To what extent are these expectations realized in the actual behavior of Soviet children? Our data on this question come from two sources: unstructured observations and impressions recorded in field notes; and systematic investigations carried out with comparable groups of children from the Soviet Union, the United States, and other countries.

The results of unstructured observations can be conveniently summarized by the following excerpt from an interim research report made at the International Congress of Psychology in 1963. Subsequent visits have served only to confirm the earlier description:

What impressed this observer, like others before him, about Soviet youngsters, especially those attending schools of the new type, was their "good behavior." In their external actions, they are well-mannered, attentive, and industrious. In informal conversations, they reveal a strong motivation to learn, a readiness to serve their society, and —in general—ironically enough for a culture committed to a materialistic philosophy, what can only be described as an idealistic attitude toward life. In keeping with this general orientation, relationships with parents, teachers, and upbringers are those of respectful but affectionate friendship. The discipline of the collective is accepted and regarded as justified, even when severe as judged by Western standards. On the basis not only of personal observations and reports from Soviet educators, but also from entries in the minutes of the Pioneer and Komsomol meetings which I had an opportunity to examine, it is apparent that instances of aggressiveness, violation of rules, or other antisocial behavior are genuinely rare.[19]

The results of our systematic investigations point to similar conclusions. The most relevant data come from a series of experiments, some of them still in progress, carried out with children in a number of different countries including the U.S.S.R.[20] Working with a sample of more than one hundred and fifty twelve-year-olds (six classrooms in three different schools) in each country, we placed the children in situations in which we could test their readiness to engage in morally disapproved behavior, such as cheating on a test, denying responsibility for property damage, etc. The situations were presented under three different experimental conditions, with ten "dilemmas" in each. Under the first, or *scientific* condition, the children were told that the research was being carried out by scientists under the sponsorship of a national scientific body (e.g., the National Science Foundation in the United States, the Academy of Sciences in the U.S.S.R.). They were informed that their responses would not be revealed to anyone whom they knew, such as parents, teachers, or fellow pupils. Even the scientists would be unaware of the behavior of particular individuals, since the data would be punched on cards, and analyzed by computers in terms of group averages. In the second, or *adult* condition, the children were asked to participate in another series, the results of which would be posted on a chart and shown to parents and teachers at a special PTA meeting. The last, or *peer* condition, was similar to the preceding. The children were asked whether they were interested in knowing how "kids" acted in situations like this. In response to the invariable "yes," we then offered to present still another series, with the understanding that the posted results would be shown only to the children themselves.

The results indicate that, under all three conditions, Soviet children are much less willing to engage in antisocial behavior than their age-mates in three Western countries (the United States, England, and West Germany). In addition, the effect of the peer group was quite different in the Soviet Union and the United States. When told that their classmates would know of their actions, American children were even more inclined to take part in misconduct. Soviet youngsters showed just the opposite tendency. In fact, their classmates were about as effective as parents and teachers in decreasing misbehavior.

In a second experiment, we compared the reactions of Russian children enrolled in three ordinary day schools (two classes in each) with responses of pupils in the same grade (the fifth, which means an average age of twelve) from three different *internats* or boarding schools (again two classes in each). As "schools of the new type," these institutions place even greater emphasis on collectivism and on the development of Communist morality. In keeping with this emphasis, the boarding school pupils were even more resistant to antisocial behavior than their age-mates in the regular schools, and showed an even smaller discrepancy in reaction to pressure from peers *versus* adults.

A third study sought to assess this special impact of collective discipline in schools of the new type while holding constant the factor of living away from home. Specifically, the responses of Soviet boarding school pupils (again about twelve years old) were compared with those of several hundred age-mates in children's homes in Switzerland, a nation in which the theory and practice of group upbringing have been well developed since the days of Johann Pestalozzi, but in the absence—and indeed in explicit rejection—of the collective approach.[21] The experiment required each child to say what he would do if he learned that a classmate or friend had engaged in some form of misconduct. Twenty-one situations were presented ranging from minor misdeeds or annoying habits (e.g., littering, eating sloppily) to more serious offenses such as breaking rules, hurting other children, insulting teachers, damaging property, cheating on an important exam, or taking things belonging to others. In each situation the child could choose one of four courses of action:

> tell a grown-up so that he could put a stop to it.
> tell the other kids so that they could do something about it.
> talk to the child himself and tell him he should not do it.
> do nothing about it since it really is none of his business.

After the experiment had been conducted (but before examining the results), we had asked the upbringers in each country what responses they hoped the children had given. (The upbringers did not participate in the administration of the experiment, and were not told until afterward what it had involved.) Soviet educators were generally agreed that, at the age level in question (eleven to thirteen years), children should first take personal initiative in correcting the behavior of their friends and classmates, and then call on the collective only if this effort failed. Among Swiss staff members there was no clear consensus on the issue. The actual research results revealed a rather different pattern for children in the two countries. In the great majority of instances (75 per cent), the Soviet youngsters reacted by saying that they themselves would talk to the offender. In contrast, only a third of the Swiss children gave this response. To the extent that there was a preferred response among the latter, it was to tell an adult (39 per cent). Only 11 per cent of Soviet children preferred this alternative. Russian youngsters were more willing than Swiss to invoke the help of other children in dealing with misconduct (12 per cent in comparison with 6 per cent), particularly if the offense involved hurting another child or discourtesy to a teacher. But an even sharper discrepancy was apparent with respect to the remaining option: "Do nothing, since it is none of my business." Whereas 20 per cent of Swiss children chose to look the other way, less than one per cent of Soviet pupils picked this alternative.

Taken together, the results of these three studies strongly indicate that collective upbringing does achieve some of its intended effects—at least at the school age level. Not only does the peer group in the U.S.S.R. act to support behavior consistent with the values of the adult society, but it also succeeds in inducing its members to take personal initiative and responsibility for developing and maintaining such behavior in others.

In the light of our earlier analysis, one other feature of the research results deserves comment. Of the various groups of boys and girls in the several countries in which we have worked (now numbering half a dozen), the Soviet girls show both the highest level of commitment to adult standards and the least individual variation within the classroom. In other words, our empirical findings confirm the impression that it is Soviet girls in particular who support the society's values, and—both as individuals and in their collectives—exert pressure on others to conform to standards of good behavior. Though Soviet boys are not so committed as the girls, their responses, under all experimental conditions, were considerably more "adult-oriented" than those of their Western counterparts.

In summary, considering both the observational and experimental data, it would seem that Soviet methods of upbringing, both within and outside the family, are accomplishing their desired objectives. The children appear to be obedient; they are also self-disciplined, at least at the level of the collective. But what about the individual? Is he capable of self-discipline when self-determination is required, particularly when the situation demands going it alone, perhaps in opposition to the group?

Some light is shed on this issue by a study conducted by Robert R. Rodgers, Bronfenbrenner, and Edward C. Devereux, Jr., on standards of social behavior among school children in four cultures: England, Switzerland, the Soviet Union and the United States.[22] Again the subjects were sixth-graders, with those from Switzerland and the U.S.S.R. coming from boarding schools and children's homes. The results showed that Soviet youngsters placed stronger emphasis than any other group on overt propriety, such as being clean, orderly, and well-mannered, but gave less weight than the subjects from the other countries to telling the truth and seeking intellectual understanding.

This result is, of course, not incompatible with the other data we have reported highlighting the obedience of Russian children. Indeed, another way of describing our findings as a whole is to say that, from a cross-cultural perspective, Soviet children, in the process of growing up, are confronted with fewer divergent views both within and outside the family and, in consequence, conform more completely to a more homogeneous set of standards.

Portents of Change

Consonant as such a conclusion is with our data—as well as with commonly held stereotypes of the U.S.S.R.—to accept the foregoing statement as an appropriate conclusion is to do injustice both to Soviet society, and perhaps to our own. For Soviet society is changing, at least at the level of social institutions, if not of values. For example, with respect to families, the equalized sex ratio at ages below thirty-five means that father-absent homes are becoming far less frequent. And with regard to communal upbringing, Khrushchev's successors appear to be much less enthusiastic than he about the panacean powers of the schools of the new type. In sharp contrast to the frequent and fervid pronouncements about them a decade ago, the *internats* and schools of the prolonged day are scarcely mentioned in public statements by high Soviet officials; and there has apparently been a sharp decrease in new construction, particularly of the boarding schools. What accounts for the change in heart? Economic pressure is surely a factor, for these kinds of facilities are expensive both to build and to operate, but other considerations would seem to have played a role as well. Some of them were already apparent at the time the schools of the new type were introduced. Although the widespread expansion of institutional upbringing was enthusiastically welcomed by some Communist ideologues, there were also expressions of criticism and dissatisfaction both on the part of professionals and the general public. A case in point is provided by the strong reaction to an article published in the popular literary journal *Novy Mir* by a distinguished Soviet academician, economic planner, and "old Bolshevik," Stanislav Gustavovich Strumilin. His central conceptions are contained in the following excerpts:

Under Soviet conditions it is especially noticeable how the lot of the woman worker is being lightened. She can work in one factory, her husband in another, both can eat in a communal dining facility while sending their children to nurseries, kindergartens and boarding schools. . . . Recognizing that communal forms of upbringing have an unquestionable superiority over all others, we are faced with the task in the immediate years ahead of expanding the network of such institutions at such a pace that within fifteen to twenty years they are available—from cradle to graduation—to the entire population of the country. Every Soviet citizen, upon leaving the maternity home, will be sent to a nursery; from there to a kindergarten maintained day and night; then to a boarding school from which he will enter independent life. . . .

. . . The question arises: will not this kind of early separation of the child from his family be too painful an experience both for parents and for infants who are so dependent on maternal affection?

This question may be answered as follows: the communal organization of upbringing in no sense requires full separation of the child from the parents . . . and surely no one will keep a mother from visiting her children when she is not working, from looking into the children's area, located in the same building in which she works, as often as it is permitted by the established schedule.

The "vitamins of love" are necessary for all children in equal measure, . . . but the easiest way to satisfy this need is through the system of communal institutions of up-bringing.

. . . The former family is reduced to the married couple, . . . and when these contracted families recognize that it is not sensible to expend so much work on maintaining an independent household just for two people, the family as an *economic* unit, having fused with other families and become incorporated into a larger economic collective, will dissolve within the context of the future social commune.[23]

The article provoked so many critical letters from readers that the editors of *Novy Mir* turned to a prominent psychologist, V. N. Kolbanovsky, to summarize the popular reaction and to express his own views on the issues raised. Obviously reflecting prevailing public sentiment, Professor Kolbanovsky challenged Strumilin's position on several counts. He began by questioning whether it was necessary "to deprive the family of that joy which is given by well-brought-up children."

Already the Soviet work days are reduced to six or seven hours, and this is only the beginning. When one adds to this the fact that communal services are relieving the family of many household chores, it becomes clear that parents will be having more time to spend in bringing up their children. Moreover the family has certain unique qualifications for this job inhering in the affectional relationship between its members.

Finally, Kolbanovsky charged, "Children would be deprived indeed, if they had to survive solely on miserly 'vitamins of love' without being able to give anything back in return." He concluded by acknowledging that communal upbringing had its proper and important place in the Soviet way of life, "but this in no sense implies that the family is to be alienated from the process of rearing children. . . . the Party has never considered it possible to supplant the family by society."[24]

Similar views were expressed by a number of prominent Soviet educators and social scientists including A. G. Kharchev,

N. Solovev, and A. Levshin.[25] A particularly strong case for the family was made in the writings of the sociologist Kharchev, who emphasized the unique, irreplaceable role of parental relationships in developing the emotional life of the child. In this connection he cited results of a Soviet study showing that children brought up exclusively in institutional settings, seemingly under the best of physical conditions, were at risk of being deprived of necessary "psychological stimulation."

> By virtue of its specificity, the non-repeatable nature of the influence of the family on the child constitutes an essential factor for normal child rearing. Children brought up without the participation of the family are at far greater risk of one-sided or retarded development than those who are members of family collectives.[26]

At the same time, the popular press reflected both puzzlement and public concern. An example is provided by an article in *Pravda* written by a woman reporter. She described a visit to a boarding school in Moscow. Under a window she saw a young mother who, having missed the regular visiting hours, was hoping to catch a glimpse of her son or hear his voice. The correspondent found this incident disturbing:

> Once again my thoughts returned to that mother standing beneath the window of the boarding school. I cannot get her out of my mind. This is not a bad boarding school. But just the same, a mother's heart begins to yearn. Can we really reproach that heart for sentimentality? Of course not. A human being—especially a mother—is so constructed that she longs to warm her own child with her love and to be warmed herself by its side.[27]

Nor was the reaction particular to mothers. Solovev in his *The Family in Soviet Society* quoted a factory worker as saying:

> We have a great need for boarding nurseries, but the fact that my son is becoming alienated from me is so painful that I can't even talk about it. I call him, "Sasha, my son." But he just runs away. No! I have to spend at least an hour or two each day with my son. Otherwise, it's impossible; otherwise, I can't stand it.[28]

But in Soviet society (as in our own) neither the pronouncements of professional experts nor the complaints of parents can be viewed as major determinants of social change. Such change is more likely to be affected by objective factors of the type mentioned earlier: the equalizing of the sex ratio in the population, the increase in leisure time made possible by shorter working hours, and, above all, the easing of the housing shortage. If our analysis is correct, all of these institutional changes should have the effect of enhancing the role of the family in the upbringing of the child and, in particular, strengthening the father as a counterweight to maternal overprotectiveness and "love-oriented" discipline. Unless Russian fathers are altogether different from those in America,[29] Germany,[30] and England,[31] they will differ from their wives in greater use of direct methods of discipline (in contrast to "withdrawal of love") and in being more task-oriented in their relations with the child, approaches which tend to promote the development of achievement and independence.

But there are changes to be seen in the behavior of Russian mothers as well. On a number of occasions, the author had opportunity to observe the behavior of the new generation of young mothers with their children, and was struck by the contrast with the traditional pattern. The following excerpt from the field notes provides a case in point.

The plane was leaving Tashkent for Alma-Ata in a few moments. As I stepped aboard, I saw an empty seat next to a young mother with her baby, and seized the opportunity. The child was about six months of age. I was struck by the way in which the mother held it—the infant's upper body away from her own. There was more of the unexpected to follow. As we got into conversation, the child began to fuss; the mother, without turning her head, plumped a chocolate into the baby's mouth and continued to talk about herself. She and her husband were students at the University in Tashkent, she said. She was a chemist, he a mathematician. The little girl kept fussing, but the mother did not speak to her or even pull her close. I had to suppress an impulse to take her up myself. The inhibition was strongly reinforced by what was happening. Every time the child whimpered, another chocolate had been popped into her mouth so that by now her face, arms, and dress were streaked with brown. Still the mother did nothing.

I reached into my jacket pocket. On the plane to Moscow, I had helped myself generously from the box of "wash-and-dries." Taking one out of my pocket. I explained its purpose and offered it to my companion. "*Spasibo*," she said with a smile, and, undoing the wrapper and sniffing the fragrance, proceeded, with slow, measured strokes, to wipe her own brow.

I learned later the purpose of her journey. In Tashkent where she and her husband lived, there were no places left in the public nurseries. The situation in Alma-Ata was far better, and she was flying there to enroll her baby. Some relatives were living there. Besides it was only a couple of hours by jet so that it would be easy to get up to see the baby on occasional weekends.

Clearly this is not a good mother as judged by the standards of Soviet upbringing. Equally clearly, she is an exception to the rule. But I observed others like her—not so extreme to be sure—among the rising generation of married students and young professionals. If this is indeed a trend, it would represent a manifestation in Soviet society, admittedly on a much smaller scale, of the same disruptive process we have seen operating massively on the American scene in which urbanization, increased physical and social mobility, and other institutional changes are seriously weakening the power of the family as a socializing agent.

But in the Soviet Union an effort has been made to compensate for such limitation through the widespread use of collective upbringing. Are there changes that can be observed or anticipated in this important Soviet sphere? Without question, the most significant development has been the new emphasis in the work of Soviet educational experts and researchers on the relation between the collective and the individual. The most outspoken of these writers criticized Soviet educational practices for a one-sided interpretation of collective upbringing. The following excerpts from an influential paper by L. I. Novikova[32] define the issue:

> A substantial deficiency of our children's collective con-
> sists of the uniformity of the internal relations determin-
> ing the life experiences of the child. Relations in school are
> most often limited to the sphere of task-oriented relations.
> It is precisely these which in the first instance are devel-
> oped by teachers. These are relations of mutual depend-
> ence, mutual responsibility, mutual control, subordination
> and commanding, and intolerance to persons interfering
> with the common tasks. These are very important relations
> determining one of the essential aspects of the moral side
> of man. But one cannot include under them all of the vari-
> eties of human relationships. By developing primarily the
> task-oriented aspects of human relationships in the chil-
> dren's collective and allowing other characteristics to de-
> velop as they may, we in the last analysis impoverish the
> personality of the child.

> Although the collective represents a means for moral
> education, it demands from each person a definite form of
> behavior corresponding to commonly accepted norms.
> Here are created not only the conditions essential for the
> harmonious development of personality, but there also
> arise social attitudes against those who do not wish to im-
> prove themselves. . . . But if every year we shall be obtain-
> ing more highly developed people but all of the same type,
> then this will be of little profit either to society or to per-
> sonality. Socialist society is interested in original persons
> capable of revolution in the spheres of science, technology,
> and the organization of production. And the personality is
> interested in developing to the full those capacities with
> which it has been endowed by nature. And these capacities
> are by no means the same in all people. Thus we have an
> instance in which the interests of socialist society and per-
> sonality completely coincide.[33]

How did this one-sidedness come about? Novikova offers a historical interpretation:

The function of the collective in relation to the individual in socialist society was expressed differently at different periods of socialist development. In the early years, in connection with the revolutionary reorganization of society, the upbringing functions of the collective were connected mainly with the development of revolutionary self-consciousness among its members, with the formation of the civic outlook. Having just mobilized all of its internal resources, the society could direct all the will and consciousness of its members on overcoming the difficulties connected with the war and the destruction of the economy. It was necessary to create those minimal material and spiritual conditions for all without which the individual is unable not only to develop but even to exist. It is natural that in that period the society was not able to provide adequate conditions for the many-sided development of each person.

At the present time the solution of problems confronting the society depends in significant measure on the effectiveness of the process of forming personalities, personalities that are not only active socially and politically but also developed in all respects, not only ready to devote all their strength to the service of the Motherland, but also knowing how to find a position in society which permits the realization of all their individual potentialities, permitting them to realize with maximal effectiveness the individual abilities, talents, and gifts. If earlier we were confronted with the problem of creating that type of collective which could insure the necessary conditions for the existence of all its members, then today we have to discover how to create the kind of collective which will insure the most full and many-sided development of each person.[34]

It is significant that Novikova's article was published as "an aid for party instruction," and that the foregoing passages were cited with approval and elaborated upon in a definitive essay on "The Development of the Basic Ideas of Soviet Pedagogy" by F. F. Korolev,[35] a leading Soviet educator and Director of the

Institute on the Theory and History of Pedagogy. Korolev goes on to say that, in contrast to the one-sidedness of Soviet educational practice in the preceding period, "In the 1960's the problem of the collective and the individual is beginning to be resolved in a new way. Precisely during this period there has been a striking growth of investigations concerned with the analysis of this problem." And, indeed, during my most recent visits to Soviet research centers in 1967 and 1968, I was told repeatedly of the organization of projects and even entire laboratories devoted to this topic. These studies are still in progress. It will be a matter of great interest to learn of the results and, what is more important, their effect on actual practice. At least, as of 1968, the new emphasis on the importance of developing the individual personality had not yet been reflected in the concrete procedures recommended in manuals for teachers, upbringers, and youth-group workers.

Nevertheless, it is clear, as in other spheres of Soviet life, Soviet upbringing is showing signs of flexibility. In particular, both within and outside the family, there is a shift away from features which foster dependency and conformity, toward new configurations more conducive to the emergence of individuality and independence. To the extent that these changes reflect and reinforce developments in Soviet society at large, we may anticipate some reduction in Soviet life generally of the primacy of the collective and its powerful sanctions against deviance in word or action.

But reduction does not mean radical change. The basic patterns of Soviet upbringing, both within the family and in collective settings, are likely to endure for some time to come. Though the young Soviet mother may not be so affectionate and solicitous as her own mother and grandmother were, she still commonly responds to her child's disobedience with a hurt look and studied coldness. And, as we have seen, she may be even more eager than her parents to enroll her child in nursery so that she can resume her studies or her job, for there is every indication that the Soviet Union will continue to be a nation of working mothers. So long as this is the case, all-day nurseries, schools of the prolonged day, Pioneer palaces, camps, and other communal facilities for children will continue to be popular.

An ironic witness for this prediction is found in the same newspaperwoman who could not forget the mother waiting longingly beneath the window of her son's boarding school. The journalist sees a solution to the problem.

> And you know what I'm dreaming about? . . . A house. . . . In the house families are living. Next door or not far away there is a building in which a boarding school complex is situated. Children from nursery to senior high school age spend their entire day there, but in the evening, when their parents come home from work, they meet with their children. On those evenings when the parents are busy with civic obligations or go to the theater, the children remain in their boarding school. They stay there too when Mother goes to a hospital or travels somewhere in connection with her job. . . .
>
> I know that this is the dream of many and many a mother. . . .
>
> Perhaps, when we are more prosperous, when we build communism, we shall live exactly so![36]

Yes, perhaps exactly so.

In any event, whatever the future may hold, we have every reason to expect that Soviet society will continue to rely heavily on communal facilities for the care and education of children. And in all of these institutions, as well as in the regular schools, the well-proven techniques of collective upbringing, even if applied with greater tolerance for individual needs, will continue to be used.

All of this suggests that Soviet children of the future will continue to be more conforming than our own. But this also means that they will be less anti-adult, rebellious, aggressive, and delinquent. During our family sojourns in the U.S.S.R., we learned to our surprise and pleasure that the streets of Moscow and other Soviet cities were reasonably safe for women and children, by night as well as by day.

They say New York was that way once. America, too, has been changing, and so have our ways of bringing up children. We turn next to an examination of current trends in child rearing in our own society.

PART II

CHILD REARING IN AMERICA: PAST, PRESENT, AND FUTURE

4

The Unmaking of the American Child

PARTICULARLY since World War II, many changes have occurred in patterns of child rearing in the United States, but their essence may be conveyed in a single sentence: *Children used to be brought up by their parents.*

It may seem presumptuous to put that statement in the past tense. Yet it does belong to the past. Over the years, *de facto* responsibility for upbringing has shifted away from the family to other settings in the society, some of which do not recognize or accept the task. While the family still has the primary moral and legal responsibility for the character development of children, it often lacks the power or opportunity to do the job, primarily because parents and children no longer spend enough time together in those situations in which such training is possible. This is not because parents do not want to spend time with their children. It is simply that conditions have changed.

An Outmoded Past

To begin with, families used to be bigger—not in terms of more children so much as more adults—grandparents, uncles, aunts, cousins. Those relatives who did not live with you lived nearby. You often went to their house. They came as often to yours, and stayed for dinner. You knew them all, the old folks, the middle-aged, the older cousins. And they knew you. This had its good side and its bad side.

On the good side, some of these relatives were interesting people, or so you thought at the time. Uncle Charlie had been to China. Aunt Sue made the best penuche fudge on the block. Cousin Bill could read people's minds (he claimed). And they all gave you Christmas presents.

But there was the other side. You had to give them all Christmas presents. Besides, everybody minded your business. They wanted to know where you had been, where you were going, and why. And if they did not like what they heard, they said so (particularly if you had told the truth).

And it wasn't just your relatives. Everybody in the neighborhood minded your business. Again this had its two aspects.

If you walked on the railroad trestle, the 'phone would ring at your house, and your parents would know what you had done before you got back home. People on the street would tell you to button your jacket, and ask why you were not in church last Sunday. Sometimes you liked it and sometimes you didn't—but at least people *cared*.

You also had the run of the neighborhood. You were allowed to play in the park. You could go into any store, whether you bought anything or not. They would let you go out back where you watched them unpack the cartons, and hoped that one would break. At the lumber yard, they let you pick up the good scraps of wood. At the newspaper office, you could punch the linotype and burn your hand on the slugs of hot lead. And at the railroad station (they had railroad stations then), you could press the telegraph key, and send your dit-dah-dah all the way to Chicago.

Boyhood memories, to be sure. But they still have their present-day vestiges, documented systematically in the research of Professor Herbert Wright and his associates at the University of Kansas.[1] These investigators compared the daily life of children growing up in a small community with those living in larger towns. The principal difference: unlike their urban and suburban age-mates, children in a small town become well acquainted with a substantially greater number of adults in different walks of life, and are more likely to be active participants in the adult settings which they enter.

The Split Society

As the stable world of the small town has become absorbed into an ever-shifting suburbia, children are growing up in a different kind of environment. Urbanization has reduced the extended family to a nuclear one with only two adults; and the functioning neighborhood—where it has not decayed into an urban or rural slum—has withered to a small circle of friends, most of them accessible only by car or telephone. Paradoxically, the more people there are around, the fewer the opportunities for meaningful human contact. Whereas, before, the world in which the child lived consisted of a diversity of people in a diversity of settings, now for millions of American children the neighborhood is nothing but row upon row of buildings where "other people" live. One house, or apartment, is much like another—and so are the people. They all have more or less the same income, and the same way of life. But the child does not see much of that life, for all that people do in the neighborhood is to come home to it, have a drink, eat dinner, mow the lawn, watch television, and sleep. Increasingly often, today's housing projects have no stores, no shops, no services, no adults at work or play. This is the sterile world in which many of our children grow, and this is the "urban renewal" we offer to the families we would rescue from the slums.

Nowadays, neighborhood experiences available to children are extremely limited. To do anything at all—go to a movie, get an ice cream cone, go swimming, or play ball—one has to travel by car or bus. Rarely can a child see people working at their trades. Mechanics, tailors, or shopkeepers are either out of sight or unapproachable. Nor can a child listen to the gossip at the post office or on a park bench. And there are no abandoned houses, no barns, no attics to break into. It is a pretty bland world.

It does not really matter, however, for children are not at home much either. They leave early on the school bus, and it is almost supper time when they get back. And there may not be anybody home when they get there. If their mother is not working, at least part-time (and over a third of American mothers are), she is out a lot because of social obligations—not just to be with friends, but to do things for the community. The men leave in the morning before the children are up. And they do not get back until after the children have eaten supper. Fathers are often away weekends, as well as during the week.

All of this means that American parents do not spend as much time with children as they used to. Systematic evidence consistent with this conclusion comes from a survey by the author of changes in child-rearing practices in the United States over a twenty-five-year period.[2] As a basis for the analysis, data were used from some thirty studies carried out during this interval by a variety of investigators. In the original publication, the data were interpreted as indicating a trend toward universal permissiveness in parent-child relations, especially in the period after World War II. "The generalization applies in such diverse areas as oral behavior, toilet accidents, dependency, sex, aggressiveness, and freedom of movement outside the house."[3]

With the benefit of hindsight, the original author now recognizes that these same data admit of another interpretation, consistent with the trend toward permissiveness, but going beyond it; namely, the same facts could be viewed as reflecting a progressive decrease, especially in recent decades, in the amount of contact between American parents and their children.

The same conclusion is indicated by data from another perspective—that of cross-cultural research. In a comparative study of parental behavior in the United States and West Germany, Devereux, Bronfenbrenner, and George J. Suci, found, somewhat to their surprise, that German parents not only disciplined their children more, but were also more affectionate, offered more help, engaged in more joint activities, etc.[4] The differences were especially marked in the case of father with

"Dad" perceived as appreciably less of a "pal" to his kids than "*Vati*" to his "*Kinder*."

But even if Americans have to yield place to Germans in the matter of parental involvement, how do they stand in comparison to Russians? Specifically, given the prevalence of institutional upbringing in the U.S.S.R., one might conclude that American parents are closer to their children than their Russian counterparts. Paradoxically, although as yet we have no systematic data on this point, our field observations fail to support such a conclusion. Collective upbringing notwithstanding, emotional ties between Russian parents and children are, as we have seen, exceptionally strong. Maternal over-protection, overt display of physical affection, and simple companionship between parents and children appear more pronounced in Soviet society than in our own. Although, because of longer working hours and time lost in shopping and commuting, Soviet parents may spend less time at home, more of that time appears to be spent in conversation, play, and companionship with children than in American families.

In summary, whether in comparison to other contemporary cultures, or to itself over time, American society emerges as one that gives decreasing prominence to the family as a socializing agent. This development does not imply any decrease in the affection or concern of parents for their children. Nor is it a change that we have planned or wanted. Rather it is itself the by-product of a variety of social changes, all operating to decrease the prominence and power of the family in the lives of children. Urbanization, child labor laws, the abolishment of the apprentice system, commuting, centralized schools, zoning ordinances, the working mother, the experts' advice to be permissive, the seductive power of television for keeping children occupied, the delegation and professionalization of child care—all of these manifestations of progress have operated to decrease opportunity for contact between children and parents, or, for that matter, adults in general.

If a child is not with his parents or other adults, where does he spend his time? There are two answers to this question. First and foremost, he is with other children—in school, after school, over weekends, and on holidays. But even this contact is further restricted. The passing of the neighborhood school in favor of "educational advantages" made possible by consolidation, homogeneous grouping by age—and more recently by ability—has set the pattern for other activities, so that from preschool days onward a child's contacts with other children in school, camp, and neighborhood tend to be limited to youngsters of his own age and social background. Whereas invitations used to be extended to entire families, with *all* the Smiths visiting *all* the Joneses, nowadays, every social event has its segregated equivalent for every age group down to the toddlers. The children's hour has become the cocktail hour. While the adults take their drinks upstairs, the children have their "juice time" in the rumpus room downstairs.

As the foregoing example indicates, the segregation is not confined to the young. Increasingly often, housing projects, or even entire neighborhoods, cater to families at a particular stage of the life cycle or career line, and social life becomes organized on a similar basis, with the result that, at all levels, contacts become limited to persons of one's own age and station. In short, *we are coming to live in a society that is segregated not only by race and class, but also by age.*

The degree to which such segregation has developed in our society is illustrated by a full-column article on the front page of the *Wall Street Journal*. The headline runs:

A PITCH FOR KIDS: NEW GOLF LINKS
ARE FOR YOUTH ONLY

The article demonstrates how separate golf links for children are better for all concerned: crowding on private and public courses is reduced, the kids become better golfers, "because they can play more," and parents are "enthusiastic." One mother is quoted: "When we go out we drop our three children off, and they play the little course while we play the big one. . . . We're strictly a golfing family."[5]

It doesn't take children very long to learn the lesson the adult world teaches: "Don't bug us! Latch on to your peers!"

Adults vs. Peers

And, as our data indicate, that is exactly what children do. In a recently completed study by John C. Condry, Jr., Michael L. Siman, and Bronfenbrenner, 766 sixth grade children reported spending, during the weekend, an average of two to three hours a day with their parents.[6] Over the same period, they spent slightly more time than this with groups of friends, and an additional two to three hours per day with a single friend. In short, they spent about twice as much time with peers, either singly or in groups, as with their parents. Moreover, their behavior apparently reflects preference as well as practice. When asked with whom they would rather spend a free weekend afternoon, many more chose friends than parents. An analysis of sex differences revealed that, although both boys and girls spent more time with peers, girls associated more with parents (especially mothers) during weekends than did the boys. Also, the boys associated more with a group, the girls with a single friend.

In this same study, the characteristics of predominantly "peer-oriented" and "adult-oriented" children were compared, and an attempt was made to answer the question of how the peer-oriented children "got that way." An analysis of data on the child's perception of his parents, his peers, and himself led us to conclude that the "peer-oriented" youngster was more influenced by a *lack* of attention and concern at home than by the attractiveness of the peer group. In general, the peer-oriented children held rather negative views of themselves and the peer group. They also expressed a dim view of their own future. Their parents were rated as lower than those of the adult-oriented children both in the expression of affection and support, and in the exercise of discipline and control. Finally, in contrast to the adult-oriented group, the peer-oriented children report engaging in more antisocial behavior such as "doing something illegal," "playing hooky," lying, teasing other children, etc. In summary, it would seem that the peer-oriented child is more a product of parental disregard than of the attractiveness of the peer group —that he turns to his age-mates less by choice than by default. The vacuum left by the withdrawal of parents and adults from the lives of children is filled with an undesired—and possibly *undesirable*—substitute of an age-segregated peer group.

Children and Television

But there is a second context in which American children spend much of their time. And again they are propelled there in part by parental example and parental pressure. They watch television.

Television was introduced into American homes in the early nineteen-fifties, and its growth has been prodigious. The proportion of families owning television sets rose from almost none in 1950 to 90 per cent by 1960, according to Leo Bogart.[7] Our understanding of the impact of this powerful medium, however, has lagged far behind its commercial success. The average viewing time for children between the ages of six to sixteen is 22 hours per week in America, in Lotte Bailyn's study,[8] and this compares with the approximately 14 hours a week for children in Britain established by Hilde Himmelweit, A. N. Oppenheim, and Pamela Vince.[9] Thus the American child spends about as much time watching television as he spends in school, and more than in any other activity except sleep and play. Younger children tend to watch more than older children, although the differences are not great.

In a study reported by Paul A. Witty and his colleagues the averages ranged from 17 hours per week for second grade, up to 28 hours a week for sixth grade.[10] In addition, children of higher levels of social class or IQ tend to watch more television than those of lesser ability or lower social status.[11]

By the time the average child is sixteen he has watched

from 12,000 to 15,000 hours of television. In other words, he has spent the equivalent of 15 to 20 solid months, 24 hours a day, before a television screen. Accordingly, it behooves us to know of the potential effects of this powerful and omnipresent source of influence. It would be wrong to assume, from the outset, that all the effects of television are necessarily bad—or good. But it could be folly to *ignore* the possible effects and to allow this massive intrusion into the daily lives of children without at least questioning its impact. Indeed, the relevant question was posed many centuries ago by Plato:

> And shall we just carelessly allow children to hear any casual tales which may be devised by casual persons, and to receive in their minds ideas for the most part the very opposite of those which we should wish them to have when they are grown-up?[12]

We shall examine possible answers to this question shortly. For the moment, we may summarize what we have learned about the status of children in American society in a single sentence: Whereas American children used to spend much of their time with their parents and other grown-ups, more and more of their waking hours are now lived out in the world of peers and of the television screen.

What do we know about the influence of the peer group, or of television, on the lives of young children?

The Impact of Peers

The prevailing view in American society—indeed, in the West generally—has held that the child's psychological development, to the extent that it is susceptible to environmental influence, is determined almost entirely by his parents, and within the first six years of life at that. And scientific investigators—who are, of course, also products of their own culture, imbued with its tacit assumptions about human nature—have acted accordingly. Western studies of influences on personality development in childhood overwhelmingly take the form of research on parent-child relations, with the peer group, or other extra-parental influences, scarcely being considered.

In other cultures, this is not always so. A few years ago, at the International Congress of Psychology held in Moscow, the author was privileged to chair a symposium on "Social Factors in Personality Development." Of the score of papers presented at the symposium, about half were from the West (mostly American) and half were from the socialist countries (mostly Russian). Virtually without exception the Western reports dealt with parent-child relationships, while those from the Soviet Union and other East European countries focused equally ex-clusively on the influence of the peer group, that is, the chil-dren's collective.

Some relevant studies have been carried out in our own so-ciety. To begin with, we can learn something from investiga-tions of the effects of parental absence. For example, in a study by Bronfenbrenner of American adolescents from middle-class families, it was found that children who reported that their par-ents were away from home for long periods of time rated sig-nificantly lower on such characteristics as responsibility and leadership.[13] Perhaps because it was more pronounced, absence of the father was more critical than that of the mother, partic-ularly in its effect on boys. Similar results have been reported in studies of the effects of father absence among soldiers' families during World War II,[14] in homes of Norwegian sailors and whalers,[15] and households with missing fathers both in the West Indies[16] and the United States.[17] In general, father ab-sence contributes to low motivation for achievement, inability to defer immediate rewards for later benefits, low self-esteem, susceptibility to group influence (e.g., children with absent fathers are more likely to "go along with the gang"), and ju-venile delinquency. All of these effects are much more marked for boys than for girls.

The fact that father absence increases the child's suscepti-bility to group influence leads us directly to consideration of the impact of the peer group on children's attitudes and behaviors.

In particular, the psychological continuity of family and peer-collective observed in Soviet society raises the question of the nature of this same relation in our own culture. The answer to the question is reflected by the very way in which the research problem has been formulated. The relatively few studies in this area all focus on the "conflict" between family and peer group. Two investigations in the nineteen-fifties indicated that, in the age range studied (twelve-to-eighteen years), although both sources were influential, the peer group tended to outweigh parents in influencing children's values and acts.[18] A broader perspective is provided by the first (and as yet the only) comprehensive research on this question carried out by two sociologists, Charles E. Bowerman and John W. Kinch, in 1959.[19] Working with a sample of several hundred students from the fourth to the tenth grades in the Seattle school system, these investigators studied age trends in the tendency of children to turn to parents or to peers for opinion, advice, or company in various activities. In general, there was a turning point at about the seventh grade. Before that, the majority looked mainly to their parents as models, companions, and guides to behavior; thereafter, the children's peers had equal or greater influence.

Recently, Condry and Siman completed a study designed to reveal current trends in the reliance of children on parents versus peers as sources of information and opinion.[20] The results show a substantially greater percentage of peer "dependence" at every age and grade level than did Bowerman's and Kinch's study. It would appear that the shift from parents to peers as the child's major source of information occurs at an earlier time than it did a decade ago and is now much more pronounced.

In the early nineteen-sixties, the power of the peer group was documented even more dramatically by James S. Coleman in *The Adolescent Society*.[21] Coleman investigated the values and behavior of teen-agers in eight large American high schools. He reported that the aspirations and actions of American adolescents were primarily determined by the "leading crowd" in the school society. For boys in this leading crowd, the hallmark of success was glory in athletics; for girls, the popular date. Intellectual achievement was, at best, a secondary value. The most intellectually able students were not those getting the best grades. The classroom was not where the action was. The students who did well were "not really those of highest intelligence, but only the ones who were willing to work hard at a relatively unrewarded activity."[22]

The most comprehensive study relevant to these concerns was a survey, also directed by Coleman, of factors affecting educational achievement in the nation's schools.[23] The data were obtained from over six hundred thousand children in grades one to twelve in four thousand schools carefully selected to be representative of public education in the United States. An attempt was made to assess the relative contribution to the child's intellectual development (as measured by standardized intelligence and achievement tests) of the following factors:

Family background (e.g., parents' education, family size, presence in the home of reading materials, records)

School characteristics (e.g., per pupil expenditure, classroom size, laboratory and library facilities)

Teacher characteristics (e.g., background, training, years of experience, verbal skills)

Characteristics of other children in the same school (e.g., their background, academic achievement, career plans).

Of the many findings of the study, two were particularly impressive; the first entirely expected, the second somewhat surprising. The expected finding was that home background was the most important factor in determining how well the child did at school, more important than any or all aspects of the school which the child attended. This generalization, while especially true for Northern whites, applied to a lesser degree to Southern whites and Northern Negroes, and was actually reversed for Southern Negroes, for whom the characteristics of the school were more important than those of the home. It is as if the child drew sustenance from wherever it was available. When the home had more to offer, it became more determining; but when the school could provide more stimulation than the home, then the school became the more influential factor.

The second conclusion concerned the aspects of the school environment which contributed most to the child's intellectual achievement. Surprisingly enough, such items as per pupil expenditure, number of children per class, laboratory space, number of volumes in the school library, and the presence or absence of ability grouping were of little significance. Teacher qualifications accounted for some of the child's achievement. But by far the most important factor was the *characteristics of the other children attending the same school*. Specifically, if a lower-class child had schoolmates who came from advantaged homes, he did reasonably well; but if all the other children also came from deprived backgrounds, he did poorly.

What about the other side of the story? What happens to a middle-class child in a predominantly lower-class school; is he pulled down by his classmates?

According to the Coleman report itself, the answer to this question is a reassuring "No." In his analysis Coleman found a differential pattern. The academic achievement of relatively deprived groups, such as Puerto Ricans, Southern Negroes, and Mexican Americans, was indeed markedly dependent on the background characteristics of their fellow students. In contrast, more advantaged groups, such as Northern whites and Oriental Americans, appeared to be unaffected by the background of their schoolmates. This pattern of results led Coleman to conclude "that the environment provided by the student body is asymmetrical in its effects, that it has its greatest effect on those from educationally deficient backgrounds."[24] In interpreting this result, Coleman suggested that "that family background which encourages achievement reduces sensitivity to variations in school." In other words, good home background can immunize a child against debilitating effects of group contagion.

Unfortunately, Coleman's optimism appears, at the very least, to be overstated, since it can be called into question on several grounds. First, the analysis on which his conclusions were based was done solely at the level of schools, not of classrooms. In other words, it paid attention to the characteristics of the entire student body, and did not ask specifically about the backgrounds of the children who sat in the *same room*. Yet, to the extent that companions influence academic work, it is these classmates who should have the greatest impact. A subsequent re-analysis of the Coleman data, on a classroom basis, carried out for the United States Commission on Civil Rights, confirmed this expectation by showing that the beneficial effect for a disadvantaged child of being in a class with non-disadvantaged pupils increased substantially with the proportion that non-disadvantaged children represent of the class as a whole.[25] Thus those disadvantaged children who were gaining the most academically were attending classes in which the majority of pupils came from white middle-class families. Moreover, these gains were substantially greater than any attributable to teacher characteristics or quality of instruction, a finding which led the authors of the report to conclude that, "Changes in the social class or racial composition . . . would have a greater effect on student achievement and attitude than changes in school quality."[26]

Finally, pursuing this same line of inquiry one step further, Thomas F. Pettigrew, in a special re-analysis of some of Coleman's data, showed that white children in predominantly Negro schools performed, on the average, below comparable white children in predominantly white schools: furthermore, "those white children in predominantly Negro schools with close Negro friends" scored significantly lower on tests of verbal achievement than white pupils in the same school without "close Negro friends."[27]

Analogous effects appear in the sphere of social behavior as well. In a study still in progress involving 40 sixth grade classrooms in a large city, we find that the willingness of the rest of the class to engage in antisocial behavior (such as cheating on a test) is significantly increased by the presence of a small lower-class minority (in this instance, all white).

Finally, there is the evidence already cited from our own researches that the peer group has quite different effects in the Soviet Union and in the United States. In the former it operates to reinforce adult-approved patterns of conduct, whereas, in our country, it intensifies antisocial tendencies.

In summary, the effect of a peer group on the child depends on the attitudes and activities which prevail in that peer group. Where group norms emphasize academic achievement, the members perform accordingly; where the prevailing expectations call for violation of adult norms, these are as readily translated into action. In short, *social contagion is a two-way street.*

How early in life do children become susceptible to the effects of such contagion? Professor Albert Bandura and his colleagues at Stanford University have conducted some experiments which suggest that the process is already well developed at the preschool level.[28] The basic experimental design involves the following elements. The child finds himself in a familiar playroom. As if by chance, in another corner of the room there is a person playing with toys. Sometimes this is an adult (a teacher), sometimes another child. This other person behaves very aggressively. He strikes a large Bobo doll (a bouncing inflated figure), throws objects, and mutilates dolls and animal toys, using appropriate language at the same time. Later on, the experimental subject (i.e., the child who "accidentally" observed the aggressive behavior) is tested by being allowed to play in a room containing a variety of toys, including some similar to those employed by the aggressive model. Without any provocation, perfectly normal, well-adjusted preschoolers engage in aggressive acts, not only repeating what they had observed but elaborating on it. Moreover, the words and gestures accompanying the actions leave no doubt that the child is living through an emotional experience of aggressive expression.

The Impact of Television

It is inconvenient to use a live model every time. Thus it occurred to Bandura to make a film. In fact, he made two; one with a live model, a second of a cartoon cat who said and did everything the live model had said and done. The films were presented on a television set left on in a corner of the room as if by accident. When the children were tested, the television film turned out to be just as effective as real people, with the cat arousing as much aggression as the human model.[29]

As soon as Bandura's work was published, the television industry issued a statement, "Commentary on Bandura's *Look* Article," calling his conclusions into question on the interesting ground that the children had been studied "in a highly artificial situation," since no parents were present either when the television set was on or when the aggressive behavior was observed. "What a child will do under normal conditions cannot be projected from his behavior when he is carefully isolated from normal conditions and the influences of society," the statement declared.[30] Bandura was also criticized for using a Bobo doll (which is "made to be struck") and for failing to do a follow-up of his subjects after they left the laboratory. Since then, a student of Bandura's has shown that only a ten-minute exposure to an aggressive model still differentiates children in the experimental group from the control group (similar children not subjected to the experiment) six months later.[31]

Evidence for the relevance of Bandura's laboratory findings to "real life" comes from a subsequent field study by Leonard Eron, now at the University of Iowa. In a sample of more than six hundred third-graders, Eron found that the children who were rated most aggressive by their classmates were those who watched television programs involving a high degree of violence.[32]

At what age do people become immune from contagion to violence on the screen? Professor Richard Walters, of Waterloo University in Canada, and his associate, Llewellyn Thomas, showed two movie films to a group of thirty-four-year-old hospital attendants.[33] Half of these adults were shown a knife fight between two teen-agers from the moving picture *Rebel Without a Cause;* the other half saw a film depicting adolescents engaged in art work. Subsequently, all the attendants were asked to assist in carrying out an experiment on the effects of punishment in learning.

In the experiment, the attendants gave an unseen subject (presumably a patient in the hospital) an electric shock every time the subject made an error. The lever for giving shocks had settings from zero to ten. To be sure the "assistant" understood what the shocks were like, he was given several, not exceeding the level of four, before the experiment. Since nothing was said about the level of shocks to be administered, each assistant was left to make his own choice. The hospital attendants who had seen the knife-fight film gave significantly more severe shocks than those who had seen the art-work film. The same experiment was repeated with a group of twenty-year-old females. This time the sound track was turned off so that only visual cues were present. But neither the silence nor the difference in sex weakened the effect. The young women who had seen the aggressive film administered more painful shocks.

A third version of the experiment employed fifteen-year-old high school boys as subjects. With this group, the designers of the experiment wondered what would happen if no film were shown. Would the continuing emotional pressures of the everyday environment of adolescents—who see more movies and more television programs and are called on to display virility through aggressive acts in teenage gangs—provoke latent brutality comparable to that exhibited by the older people under direct stimulation of the movie of the knife fight?

The results of the experiment were sobering. Even without the suggestive power of the aggressive film to step up their feelings, the teenagers pulled the shock lever to its highest intensities (levels eight to ten). A few of the boys made remarks which suggested that they were enjoying the experience of administering pain; for example, "I bet I made that fellow jump."

A strikingly similar pattern of results is found in a series of studies by Leonard Berkowitz and his colleagues.[34] Berkowitz' research has confirmed and extended the findings reported by Bandura and Walters, and has done so utilizing still another population of subjects, college students. Once again subjects observing aggressive films reacted with more aggression than controls viewing non-aggressive or neutral material. In addition, Berkowitz demonstrates that the aggression provoked by the film is most likely to be directed at persons toward whom the subjects already feel some hostility.[35] In other words, after seeing a violent television show or movie, the viewer is most prone to "take it out on" somebody he already dislikes. Berkowitz emphasizes, however, that the target person need not be someone who has been the immediate cause of injury or frustration. Nor is the presence of a disliked person necessary for the aroused aggression to be expressed.

This fact raises an interesting question. Common belief holds that aggressive responses are most likely to be aroused when one has been mistreated. Presumably, one does not get angry without a cause. Yet a number of the experiments we have reviewed indicate that aggressive—and even cruel—behavior can be induced in a person without giving him any ground for grievance, by simply allowing him to observe aggressive behavior, purely as a bystander. One wonders. Is his reaction as great as that which would be aroused by a personal affront? And what is it about an aggressive stimulus that evokes an aggressive response? Specifically, is it the sight of the aggressor, or of his victim, that arouses one's own hostile impulses?

Answers to these questions are provided by an ingenious experiment carried out in the course of doctoral research at Stanford University by D. P. Hartman.[36] To maximize the likelihood of an aggressive reaction to a personal affront, the subjects selected for research were adolescent delinquent boys. In the first phase of the experiment, each boy "accidentally" overheard his future partner—an anonymous member of the group (actually a tape recording)— making comments about him. For half the subjects, the comments overheard were essentially neutral; for the other half, they included a number of unwarranted disparaging criticisms. In the next phase of the experiment, the boys were divided into three groups. Each group was then shown a film which portrayed two teen-agers shooting baskets on a court.

. . . In the *control* film the boys engage in an active but co-operative basketball game, whereas in the other two films the boys get into an argument that develops into a fist fight. The *pain-cues* film focuses almost exclusively on the victim's pain reactions as he is vigorously pummeled and kicked by his opponent. The *instrumental-aggression* film, on the other hand, focuses on the aggressors' responses including angry facial expressions, foot thrusts, flying fists, and aggressive verbalizations. . . .[37]

Following the procedure developed by the Canadian investigators, Hartman then asked each subject to assist in an experiment by administering shocks to his partner in the learning experiment, the same one whom he had previously overheard.

The results of the experiment are instructive in a number of respects.

First, they confirm earlier work in demonstrating that exposure to film violence induces aggressive response. Both groups who had seen the fist fight administered more severe shocks than the controls who watched only the cooperative game.

Second, although subjects previously insulted gave higher shocks than those overhearing neutral remarks, this difference was not so great as that attributable to exposure to an aggressive stimulus. Specifically, the boys who had not been offended but who had seen the filmed fist fight administered stronger shocks than those who had been insulted but had seen no filmed aggression. In short, exposure turns out to be more powerful than insult in instigating aggressive behavior.

Third, the fact that angered viewers behaved more aggressively than non-angered viewers *after* seeing filmed aggression calls seriously into question the so-called catharsis hypothesis developed from psychoanalytic theory.[38] According to this hypothesis, stimuli such as films or comic books containing aggressive material perform a function in vicariously reducing aggressive impulses. It is on this basis that some psychiatrists have recommended giving toy guns to highly aggressive children and encouraging them to see violence on television. If films do function to release hostile impulses, then the teen-agers in Hartman's experiment, especially those in the "insulted" group, should "feel better" after viewing the "fist fight" than after seeing cooperative play. In fact, the results were exactly the opposite, with the highest shocks being given by the boys who had been insulted and then shown the aggressive film.

Fourth, the effect of insult was greatest among the boys who had viewed the fist fight. Prior offense produced some increase in the control subjects, "but not of statistical magnitude."[39] In other words, it was only after the injured person was exposed to a new aggressive stimulus that he really gave vent to his anger.

Finally, *pain cues* and shots of the aggressive act were equally potent in arousing aggressive response. In other words, the sight of the suffering victim, far from reducing the aggressive reactions of the viewer, actually increased them. A similar finding emerged from the study by R. G. Geen and Berkowitz.[40] Berkowitz, in a summary of his research, says "the confederate's aggressive cue value apparently varied directly with his association with the *victim* rather than the giver of the observed aggression."[41]

The implications of these research findings for the impact of television on its viewers are obvious. Given the salience of violence in commercial television, including cartoons especially intended for children, there is every reason to believe that this mass medium is playing a significant role in generating and maintaining a high level of violence in American society, including the nation's children and youth.

But the studies speak not only to the effect of television, but to the impact of models generally, and peer group models in particular. It is not irrelevant that, in the Canadian experiments, the subjects who exhibited the highest level of aggression after seeing a film of a teenage knife fight were themselves teen-agers. The impact of peer pressure in inducing aggressive response has been nicely isolated in a study by Stanley Milgram in a variant of what has come to be known as the "Eichmann experiment."[42] Using male college students as subjects, Milgram set up a situation in which the level of shock to be administered was determined by the lowest level proposed by any one of three "assistants," two of whom were confederates of the experimenter and called for increasingly higher shocks. Even though the true subjects could keep the intensity to a minimum simply by stipulating mild shocks, they increased the degree of pain administered in response to the confederates' pressure.

Yet, as we have seen, the peer group need not necessarily act as an impetus to antisocial behavior. Among Soviet youngsters, it had just the opposite effect. Why? The answer is obvious enough. The Soviet peer group is given explicit training for exerting desired influence on its members, whereas the American peer group is not. Putting it another way, the Soviet peer group is heavily—perhaps too heavily—influenced by the adult society. In contrast, the American peer group is relatively autonomous, cut off from the adult world—a particularly salient example of segregation by age.

Looking Backward

What explains this different course of social development in two large, highly industrialized countries? With respect to the U.S.S.R., we have already indicated a series of historical factors which fostered the development of strong and widely diffused dependency relations between children and adults. In addition, the primacy of the collective in claiming loyalty and submission across age and family lines has deep roots in Russian history.

The American pattern, too, has its historical antecedents. Perhaps in the first instance these derive from the fateful separation of church and state, which, as it freed the schools of religious control, also fragmented the process of education. The primary responsibility of schools became the teaching of subject matter. Character education, or what the Russians call *vospitanie*, was left to the family and the church.

The role of the church in moral education has withered to a pallid weekly session at Sunday school. And, as we have seen, the family, primarily because of changes in the larger social order beyond its control, is no longer in a position to exercise its responsibilities. As for the school—in which the child spends most of his time—it is debarred by tradition, lack of experience, and preoccupation with subject matter from concerning itself in any major way with the child's development as a person. Questions of conduct become of legitimate concern only if they "interfere with the lesson." The vacuum, moral and emotional, created by this state of affairs is then filled—by default—on the one hand by the television screen with its daily message of commercialism and violence, and on the other by the socially isolated, age-graded peer group, with its impulsive search for thrills and its limited capacities as a humanizing agent.

It is noteworthy that, of all the countries in which my colleagues and I are working, now numbering half a dozen both in West and East, the only one which exceeds the United States in the willingness of children to engage in antisocial behavior is the nation closest to us in our Anglo-Saxon traditions of individualism. That country is England, the home of the Mods and the Rockers, the Beatles, the Rolling Stones, and our principal competitor in tabloid sensationalism, juvenile delinquency, and violence. The difference between England and America in our results is not great, but it is statistically reliable.[43] England is also the only country in our sample which shows a level of parental involvement lower than our own, with both parents— and especially fathers—showing less affection, offering less companionship, and intervening less frequently in the lives of their children.[44]

Looking Forward

In summary, it is our view that the phenomenon of segregation by age and its consequences for human behavior and development, pose problems of the greatest magnitude for the Western world in general and for American society in particular. As we read the evidence, both from our own research and that of others, we cannot escape the conclusion that, if the current trend persists, if the institutions of our society continue to remove parents, other adults, and older youth from active participation in the lives of children, and if the resulting vacuum is filled by the age-segregated peer group, *we can anticipate increased alienation, indifference, antagonism, and violence on the part of the younger generation in all segments of our society —middle-class children as well as the disadvantaged.* From this perspective, the emergence of hippyism appears as the least harmful manifestation of a process which sees its far more destructive and widespread expression in the sharp rise in rates of juvenile delinquency observed in recent years, with a substantial number of the offenders now coming from "the right side of the tracks," including some of "the best families in town."

Why should age segregation bring social disruption in its wake? The dynamics of the process are not difficult to see. However important genetic factors may be in the determination of human behavior, it is quite clear that such qualities as mutual trust, kindness, cooperation, and social responsibility cannot be insured through selective breeding; they are learned from other human beings who in some measure exhibit these qualities, value them, and strive to develop them in their children. It is a matter of social rather than biological inheritance. Or, as one of the author's teachers, Walter Fenno Dearborn, used to put it: "He's a chip off the old block—not because he was knocked off it, but because he knocked around with it." But in either case, transmission cannot take place without the active participation of the older generation. If children have contact only with their own age-mates, there is no possibility for learning culturally-established patterns of cooperation and mutual concern.

Moreover, evidence for a functional interdependence between conceptual development on the one hand, and moral and social development on the other, as demonstrated by Lee Charlotte Lee, suggests that children may be incapable of developing such patterns *de novo,* or of maintaining them in the absence of intervention by adults or already-socialized older youth.[45] Thus the bands of orphaned youngsters who roamed the Soviet Union during the early nineteen-twenties, many of whom came from good families, became notorious for acts of selfishness, callousness, and violence, and it required the genius and uncommon perseverance of a Makarenko and his dedicated staff slowly to bring about patterns of mutual trust and cooperation among the children.[46]

The necessity of responsible adult involvement in the work of children's collectives and the consequences of its absence continue to be stressed in the writings of present-day Soviet educators:

> The very concept of "children's collective" is to some degree qualified, since in the life and activity of any children's collective one always assumes the participation of adults. A collective which forms without adult involvement is not likely to endure. In those instances where it continues to exist for a prolonged period, then as a rule it gets into a blind alley. The life experience of its leaders turns out to be inadequate to hold the collective to a right course even if the goal which the children themselves have set is a proper one.[47]

But as is frequently the case, it is literature which provides us with the most revealing picture of psychological process and effect. In *Lord of the Flies,* William Golding describes the course of events among a group of pre-adolescent boys marooned on an island. Patterns of civilized human relationships, epitomized in the person of "Piggy," are as yet too shallowly rooted, and are soon destroyed by the quickly rising sadism of peer power; Piggy is brutally killed just before the adult rescuers arrive. Their first question: "Are there any adults—any grown-ups with you?"[48]

The message of the allegorical ending is clear, and, in our view, dictated no less by literary insight than the independent data of behavioral science. If adults do not once again become involved in the lives of children, there is trouble ahead for American society. New patterns of life have developed in our culture. One result of these changes has been the reduced participation of adults in the socialization of children. Although, to date, this pattern has continued to gain acceptance, there is reason to believe that it can do harm to our children and to our society. We are therefore faced with the necessity of developing a new style of socialization, one that will correct the inadequacies of our contemporary pattern of living as it is affecting our children and provide them with the opportunities for humanizing experience of which they are now bereft.

In sum, it is not a question of whether or not there will be changes in the way in which we bring up our children, but rather what direction the changes will take. Shall we continue to drift, or shall we try to determine our course? If so, which approaches are both effective and feasible? What are the forces that shape human behavior and development, and how can they be utilized for constructive ends? In our concluding chapters we examine possible answers to these questions.

5

Principles and Possibilities

IN THIS CHAPTER we seek to identify and describe the major environmental forces which can influence the behavior and development of children. In marshalling these forces, we have drawn primarily on the research findings of developmental and social psychology, with a few forages into the neighboring disciplines, on either side, of human biology and sociology. Our inventory of environmental strategies is conveniently discussed under six major headings: Conserving Biological Potential, The Potency of Models, Social Reinforcement, Intensive Relationships, Group Forces, and Superordinate Goals.

Conserving Biological Potential

SOME SOVIET APPROACHES

Several years ago, the author was privileged to serve as a member of an official exchange mission to the Soviet Union in the field of public health. The group consisted of senior medical scientists, physicians, public health officers, and a social psychologist. Through the good offices of the Ministry of Health of the U.S.S.R., we were able to observe public health services in hospitals, clinics, and even homes (two of us went along on house calls with the doctor on duty at the district dispensary). In the course of several weeks, we visited facilities in five Soviet republics, including rural as well as metropolitan areas. The general conclusion of the mission can be summed up as follows: Although the quality of medical and public health services in the Soviet Union does not come up to that found in the United States, these services are adequate and reach a far larger segment of the population at the lower socioeconomic levels, with particular attention to young children and pregnant mothers.* With respect to these latter groups, especial emphasis is placed on providing regular medical care and adequate nutrition. For example, every preschool center has one or more nurses in attendance, with a physician on call. During one winter when the author was living in Moscow with his family, oranges were selling at fifty cents apiece. Even if you were lucky enough to find a kiosk that had the fruit, very likely they would have run out by the time your turn came in the long queue. During that same winter, children in nurseries and kindergartens were receiving free oranges daily.

THE AMERICAN SCENE

Only since 1968, with the publication and dramatic presentation on television of a national report on hunger in the United States, have we become aware of the extent of nutritional deficiency in our country.[1] Such deficiency takes its greatest toll, of course, among children and pregnant mothers. A child in school cannot learn very much when his stomach growls for lack of breakfast, and there is no prospect of lunch. Far worse is the damage done to preschool children and pregnant mothers, for here the impairment is not confined to present function. It is the future development of the young child which is at stake, physically, mentally, and emotionally.

Similar considerations apply to the ravages of disease. The national health surveys carried out in connection with Project Head Start reveal a substantial prevalence of remediable infection, physical handicap, and functional disorder among children of disadvantaged families. For example, 8 per cent failed a vision screen test. More than 6 per cent were anemic. Nearly two-thirds required dental treatment. About one in forty suf-

---

* To be sure, some of the benefits of maternal care are offset by damage associated with the high rate of abortion in the U.S.S.R., in the absence of reliable contraceptives and adequate family planning programs.

fered from learning problems requiring attention by specialists.[2]

Unquestionably, the period of greatest vulnerability—and also of greatest promise for corrective action—is the first two years of life, including the months before as well as after birth. The ravages of illness and injury during this period are reflected in the rate of infant mortality. The following excerpt from a special report to the President of the United States, *Advancement of Knowledge for the Nation's Health*, indicates the scope of the problem.

The death of an infant before his first birthday is a source of increasing concern in the United States. During this first year of life the risk of dying is greater than during any other year until after age 65. It has been estimated, however, that with increased knowledge and improved services, at least 20 percent and perhaps as high as 50 percent of these deaths could be prevented. . . .

The international ranking of the United States in infant mortality has dropped steadily in the past decade. In 1955, the United States ranked eighth with a rate of 26.4 per 1,000 live births. The present rate of 24.8 now places the United States in fifteenth position among the developed countries of the world.[3]

The rate of 24.8 for the country as a whole conceals a far more disturbing fact pointed out in a recent publication of the United States Children's Bureau.

. . . The neonatal mortality rate for nonwhite infants was 64 percent above that for white infants and showed no sign of improvement. Among nonwhite infants 1–11 months, the postneonatal death rate (14.6 per 1,000 live births) was nearly triple that for white infants (5.4) in 1964.

The gap between death rates for white and nonwhite infants has become wider in recent years, increasing from 66 percent in 1950 to 90 percent in 1964. This excess represents a lag of over two decades in reducing infant losses in the nonwhite group. The 1964 mortality rate of 41.1 for nonwhite infants has not been recorded since 1941. . . .[4]

Ironically, of even higher cost to the society than the infants who die are the many more who sustain injury but survive with some disability. Of particular importance in this regard is damage associated with complications of pregnancy. In this connection, the report to the President states:

> . . . Pregnancy can no longer be considered an uneventful state, for dietary intake, drugs, environmental influences, heredity, minor illnesses, emotional stress, and social factors can have a profound effect on the well-being of the fetus. . . .[5]

Here again, the destructive impact is greatest on the poorest segments of the population. For example, a series of studies conducted in Baltimore revealed extraordinarily high rates of prematurity and prenatal damage among Negro infants.[6]

Many of these abnormalities entail neurological damage resulting in impaired intellectual function and behavioral disturbances, including hyperactivity, distractibility, and low attention span. Of particular relevance is the significant role played by paranatal and prenatal factors in the genesis of childhood reading disorders. In a retrospective comparison of hospital records, A. A. Kawi and Benjamin Pasamanick found that instances of two or more complications of pregnancy were over nine times as frequent in the records of mothers whose children later exhibited severe reading difficulties as in a control population matched on social class and other relevant variables.[7] Finally, it is a well established, though not thoroughly understood, fact that neurological disorders resulting from complications of pregnancy and birth are considerably more frequent for males than females. This differential rate has been identified as a major factor in contributing to the consistent sex differences observed in incidence of neuropsychiatric disorders and psychological disturbances in children.[8] Of special relevance in this connection is the statistic that "behavior disorders are two to three times more common in boys, reading disorders as much as eight or nine times."[9] These researchers see in "reproductive casuality" and its sequelae a major factor contributing to school retardation in Negro children generally and Negro males in particular. Organic debilities, of course, result not only in intellectual dysfunction but also in discouragement. In this manner, they play a part in evoking the expectations of failure, the readiness to give up in the face of difficulty, and the low level of aspiration observed in Negro children, especially among boys.

The foregoing analysis documents the destructive impact of discrimination at the very beginnings of life for a major segment of American society. The damage is, of course, not limited to those who are its immediate victims. Ultimately the entire society must bear the burden of supporting and rehabilitating its maimed members and, in the bargain, suffering the blows of their just anger and resentment.

The foregoing account also brings home another hard fact: The success of any program designed to foster the development of children requires as its first ingredient an intact child. As we have seen, such biological integrity can be impaired by baneful environmental forces even before the child is born. Hence the first principle for any strategy of intervention is to insure that the initial environment meets at least the minimal level for sustaining normal development. In practice, this means adequate nutrition, medical care, and circumstances of life for mother and infant. How this objective may be better achieved through the institutions of our society will be considered in the next chapter.

The Potency of Models

One of the most salient developments in American social psychology during the past decade has been what for many laymen may appear as a demonstration of the obvious; namely, children learn by watching others. Or, to put the issue in more provocative form: the behavior of others is contagious.

This second formulation highlights an important point: imitation is its own reward. As shown in the experiments by Bandura, Walters, and others described in the preceding chapter (*pages 109–115*), the child takes on the actions of the model without visible inducement or compulsion—no chocolate candies, no approving nod or smile, no discomfort or shock are needed to spur him on.

It was recognition of this fact that constituted a significant departure from earlier research on learning, in which some form of reinforcement—that is, tangible reward or punishment —was regarded as virtually indispensable for inducing rapid and enduring changes in behavior.

Fortunately, reinforcement is not indispensable. If it were, it is unlikely that a child would ever learn the multitude of complex and diverse tasks required of a socialized adult in our society. Indeed, the requirement of having a person available who will continuously monitor the child's behavior and have the power to reward and punish him is almost impossible to meet.

Moreover, in comparison with reinforcement, modeling offers a number of advantages from the point of view of training or education. It is possible, with this technique, to influence a large number of children with a single carefully-selected model, whereas direct reinforcement requires a one-to-one interaction between the teacher and learner. But there is another, perhaps more important consideration. The direct reinforcement paradigm requires waiting for the behavior to appear before it can be reinforced. If the child does not manifest the response, it cannot be rewarded or punished. In contrast, modeling provides a means for inducing a behavior pattern which might otherwise never occur. An act that is low in the child's hierarchy of responses may never appear unless elicited by a model.[10] It follows that the model can influence the child's behavior in two ways: first, by doing something which the child has never experienced before, thus inducing him to engage in new patterns of behavior; second, by doing something already in the child's repertoire, thus inducing him to engage in this particular behavior rather than in some other activity. In terms of its long-range impact on the child's behavior and development, the second of these influences is perhaps even more important than the first.

THE NATURE OF MODELING

Thus far, virtually all the experiments on modeling we have considered have dealt with only one form of behavior—aggression. With the aim of clarifying the nature and range of the phenomenon, we shall now present some other examples, beginning with sexual behavior. In an experiment by Walters and his colleagues, male subjects were shown a series of pictures of nude or almost nude women in provocative poses. The viewers were told that a moving spot of light on the film indicated the eye movements of a previous subject. For half the group, the spot of light hovered over the pictured bodies focusing on the breast and genital areas. For the control group, the spot of light appeared in the background of the picture. Later, the subjects' own eye movements were recorded. Those who had been exposed to the "uninhibited" model spent more time looking at the nude bodies than did the control group.[11] Thus, even when the original action itself is not observed, being shown what other people have done can be a powerful determinant of behavior.

The experiments on aggression and sex, along with others on violation of prohibitions,[12] have in common the element of "eating forbidden fruit." The question arises whether modeling is equally effective when the behavior to be adopted involves control or adherence to standards rather than disinhibition of suppressed desires. A number of studies indicate that the potency of models is not limited solely to "release reactions." To begin with, a number of the aggression experiments (e.g., one by Bandura, Dorothea Ross, and Sheila Ross[13]) included in the research design a third group in which the adult model displayed "inhibited and non-aggressive behavior." Even when compared with the "no-model" control group, these children showed fewer aggressive responses and more of the actions previously engaged in by their peaceful model. Other studies by the same trio and by Bandura alone demonstrate that seeing a model punished has the effect of *suppressing* the behavior in question,[14] and this inhibition occurs even when the model is first seen being rewarded and then punished.[15] In one of these researches, using twelve- to fourteen-year-old boys as subjects, peer models were shown to be more effective than either a nurturant or prohibitive adult in inhibiting play with a desired toy.[16] This study provides one of the few tests of the relative power of peers and adults, although it is confounded by the fact that the adults did not act as "models" but rather forbade playing with the desired toy.

In a different sphere of behavior, a series of studies have illustrated the ability of a model to induce the adoption of a high standard of self-reward, even when doing so results in a lowered opinion of one's self.[17] Finally, Walter Mischel and his colleagues demonstrated that watching a model postpone receiving a reward for performance led the subject to display similar deferral of gratification.[18] This last finding has particular relevance to work with the culturally deprived, since the inability to delay reward is often cited as characteristic of this group, serving as a handicap both for educational achievement and for getting and keeping a job.[19]

Although all of the above studies demonstrate that modeling can be used to induce inhibition and control of behavior, these results should be tempered with a note of caution. Exposure to models who exhibit self-restraint, or who are punished for violating prohibitions does not always suffice to inhibit or even depress the subject's response,[20] especially under conditions of extreme provocation.[21] In other words, it appears doubtful that observing a model behaving responsibly or being punished for misconduct can serve as a powerful enough deterrent to dissuade a child from so enticing a prospect as breaking windows or playing hooky, especially when all his friends are urging him to join in. In short, if placed in competition, sin may well prove more seductive than self-control.

But the release or control of selfish or suppressed desires does not exhaust the repertoire of human behavior. It is regrettable that the research on modeling to date has been concentrated within these domains to the relative neglect of other areas; for example, exploring possibilities for inducing such constructive modes of response as performing high order skills, engaging in artistic expression, or helping others. Recently, a few studies of this sort have been carried out—most of them with adults as subjects—and have yielded impressive results. For example, in one experiment called "Lady in Distress," the test situation involved a young girl standing by a car parked on the roadside with a flat tire and inflated spare in conspicuous view.[22] In the experimental condition, a second car in a similar situation was stationed a quarter-mile ahead of the first, but with the girl watching a male engaged in changing the tire. In the control condition, no such "helpful model" was in view. Over a 2½-hour period, with no difference in the number of cars traveling the road, there were 35 offers of help under the control condition, 58 under the influence of the model. Similar facilitating effects were obtained by having a model deposit contributions in a Salvation Army kettle, or rendering help to a student computing arithmetic problems.[23] Finally, the only experiment we have been able to find with children as subjects similarly demonstrates the potency of an altruistic model: elementary school pupils were more likely to donate highly-valued gift certificates to residents of a fictitious orphanage if they had seen an adult do so.[24]

Although the critical comparative experiment is yet to be done, it would appear that altruistic activities can be made as visible and enticing as expressions of aggression and self-indulgence. Indeed, at a practical level, this is what the Russians appear to have done in exposing young children to the "shining example" of their older classmates. It is yet to be shown that virtue in action is any less contagious than sin.

In all of the foregoing examples, the operational definition of modeling has been the actual performance by the subject of an act concretely or symbolically similar to that previously exhibited by a model. It is important to recognize that this final outcome implies a two-phase process, involving first *acquisition* and then *performance*. A child may "acquire" a given behavior or pattern of response (i.e., have it in memory), and yet may not have the occasion, ability, or desire to display what he has observed. Thus, he learns from the television screen just how to shoot a gun, but he may not actually shoot a gun until he gets one in his hands, decides to pull the trigger, and finds that he is able to do so. Thus the conditions for acquisition of a response may not be sufficient for its performance.

An understanding of this two-phase process points to the source of a common error in analyzing the behavior of both children and adults. Too often a person's failure to *perform* an act is taken as evidence for inadequate learning. So defined, the task becomes one of "teaching" the ignorant one *how* to act correctly—such teaching often taking the form of continued repetition of the behavior in question. If one utilizes the distinction between *acquisition* and *performance*, however, a clearer picture often emerges which implies quite different remedial action. Thus if we know a child has had sufficient opportunity to observe and acquire a behavioral sequence, and we know he is physically capable of performing the act but does not do so, then it is reasonable to assume that it is motivation which is lacking. The appropriate countermeasure then involves increasing the subjective value of the desired act relative to any competing response tendencies he might have, rather than having the model senselessly repeat an already redundant sequence of behavior.

MODELING *vs.* IMITATION

Having examined the phenomenon of modeling with respect to a wide range of behaviors, we are now in a position to speak to a question which has perhaps already nettled our reader. Why the term "modeling?" Would not the more familiar concept of "imitation" do just as well? How is modeling different from "monkey see, monkey do"?

The answer to this question is provided by one of the researches with which we are already familiar: the series of experiments by Walters and his colleagues on the aggression-inducing power of the knife scene from the film *Rebel Without a Cause*. The outcome measure in these studies, it will be recalled, was the severity of the shock which the subject administered to the alleged "learner" behind the screen, *not* the subject's use of a knife in attacking a personal rival. In other words, at the level of concrete action, the subject was not mimicking the behavior of the teen-agers in the film. Rather he was taking on their expressed motivations as a model for his own, and then adapting his concrete actions to the conditions of a new and different situation presented by the fictional experiment. In short, modeling goes beyond mimicry in implying the adoption of behaviors which are *symbolic equivalents* of the behavior engaged in by the model. As the experiments in this area show, although many of the particular acts exhibited by the subject are identical with those of the model, many others are not, but they express the same "mood." This point is nicely documented in one of the experiments on film-mediated aggression by Bandura, Ross, and Ross, in which a distinction was made between imitative and non-imitative aggression.[25] The former category included only exact replicas of the aggressive model's actions; the latter, other expressions of aggression not actually contained in the model's repertoire. The results showed that children exposed to an aggressive model on film, when compared with controls, showed a significant increase in *both* categories.

FACTORS AFFECTING THE MODELING PROCESS

What are the circumstances under which modeling is most likely to occur? How can one enhance the effectiveness of the process? To answer these questions, it is useful to distinguish three sets of conditions affecting the modeling process: (*1*) characteristics of the subject; (*2*) characteristics of the stimulus act; and (*3*) characteristics of the model.

Characteristics of the subject.   Before a child can be influenced by a model he must obviously possess certain capacities. Thus he must be able to perceive the stimulus act, and to perform that same act or other behaviors expressive of the same emotional state. Since such abilities are primarily a function of his stage of psychological development, and are not immediately influenceable by the modeling situation, we shall, for the purposes of this discussion, regard them as given.

But in addition to ability, there is the problem of motivation; the child must be interested in observing the model, in learning the observed behavior, and then in performing that behavior or some related act. The usual explanation for the child's readiness to take on the characteristics of the model is based on a prior history of reinforcement;[26] that is, from earliest years children tend to be rewarded for imitating the behavior of the significant persons in their lives. Any act or utterance which resembles that of another important person, especially a parent, tends to evoke a positive response. As a result, a child learns to attend to and duplicate the behavior of those about him so that modeling becomes its own reward.

Studies purporting to demonstrate such a "generalized imitative set" of responding have done so by showing that nonreinforced imitative responses are often acquired once an imitation-reinforcement sequence has been established.[27] More research is needed to clarify this issue, however, since the above studies are susceptible to an alternative explanation.[28]

Presumably, then, children differ in their susceptibility to modeling as a function of their prior history of reinforcement for such response. Although there is no direct evidence on the point, some support comes from a study by Reuben M. Baron showing that subjects most responsive to reinforcement are those who experienced considerable reinforcement in the past.[29] In any event, to the extent that it is dependent on the child's past development, susceptibility to modeling—like capacity to perceive and respond—must, for the purposes of our discussion, be treated as given.

But even if motivation is potentially present, it must be aroused if it is to affect the child's behavior. As we shall see, this level of arousal, or counteractive inhibition, depends in significant degree on external stimuli.

Characteristics of the stimulus act.   To begin with, complex sequences of behavior are more easily learned if they can be broken down into smaller bits or components, with a separate label attached to each.[30] For example, as the model goes through a series of actions he calls out a name for each one. In addition, the relation of one act to the next in the sequence exhibited by the model becomes important. Thus the optimal strategy is one in which the child participates in progressively more complex patterns of reciprocal interaction initiated and paced by the model—for example, conversation that gradually invokes wider vocabulary and complexity of structure, or a series of games involving increasing complexity of skill, etc.

Characteristics of the model.   Finally, we come to the area of greatest potential for influencing the modeling process. The effectiveness of that process has been shown to vary appreciably with properties of the model. Specifically:

(1) *The potency of the model increases with the extent to which the model is perceived as possessing a high degree of competence, status, and control over resources.*[31] For example, in an experiment by Bandura, Ross, and Ross, two different adult models were used simultaneously: one was called the *consumer;* the other, the *controller.*[32] In one experiment, the controller, in the presence of the child, proceeded to shower the consumer with praise and gifts, including mechanical toys, dolls, and fruit juice from an automatic soda dispenser. The controller ran the show, giving directions and using equipment, all for the benefit of the consumer. At the end he offered to provide the consumer with still more dazzling gifts, such as a bicycle. The second experimental condition was identical except that the child, rather than the other adult, was the recipient of praise and largesse. Two major research questions were asked: which model would prove more effective, the controller or the consumer; would more modeling occur when the reinforcement was given to the child or to a third party?

The answer to the first question was unequivocal. Under both experimental conditions, the controller clearly served as a more powerful model than the consumer. But direct reinforcement of the child showed no reliable advantage over reinforcement of the consumer. In other words, the status of the model emerged as a more powerful factor than the degree of reinforcement received by the child.

(2) *The inductive power of the model increases with the degree of prior nurturance or reward exhibited by the model.*[33] Taken in conjunction with the foregoing principle, this gener-

alization has some important implications. To begin with, it must be recognized that the power, status, and rewarding quality of the model are defined through the eyes of the child. In other words, the most potent models in his life are the persons whom he perceives as major sources of support and control. This consideration leads us to our third proposition.

(3) *The most "contagious" models for the child are likely to be those who are the major sources of support and control in his environment; namely, his parents, playmates, and older children and adults who play a prominent role in his everyday life.* Unfortunately, as yet little research has been specifically devoted to the relative potency as models of parents, peers, relatives, older children, teachers, strange adults, etc. The general studies on the influence of family and peer group reviewed in this volume and elsewhere, however, give strong support to this proposition.[34]

(4) *The inductive power of the model increases with the degree to which the person perceives the model as similar to himself.* An experiment specifically designed to test this relationship has been carried out at the University of Minnesota.[35] Boy Scouts, ranging in age from eleven to fourteen, observed a film of a twelve-and-a-half-year-old-boy playing a war-strategy game. For half the cases, the boy was described as "a Boy Scout just like you," living in the same city and having interests and skills overlapping with those previously reported by each subject. For the remaining cases, the model was described as "living in a state far away from here," not a Scout, going to a different kind of school, and having different interests. After seeing the film, the subjects were given an opportunity to play the war game themselves. Modeling was measured by the similarity in actions and equipment used by the subject and the boy depicted on the film. As anticipated, the children who were told that the model was like themselves showed a higher number of spontaneous imitative responses, were more likely to reproduce the arrangement of pieces at the end of the game, and were able to recall more of the actions of the model than boys whose characteristics differed from those ascribed to the child in the film.

Analogous findings have been obtained with respect to attitude as distinguished from overt behavior; junior high school boys adopted more of the sea-diving preferences of a deep-sea diver portrayed as similar to them in background than of a diver described as dissimilar.[36] Several other studies provide additional support for the same hypothesis.[37] The finding mentioned earlier demonstrating the greater potency of peers over adults as models for evoking resistance to temptation in children is, of course, also in accord with the principle.

(5) *Several models, exhibiting similar behavior, are more powerful inducers of change than a single model.* Several of Bandura's experiments have confirmed this hypothesis.[38]

(6) *The potency of the model is enhanced when the behavior exhibited is a salient feature in the actions of a group of which the child already is or aspires to be a member.* In part this proposition follows from the preceding. In addition it is supported by the research on group conformity summarized in the previous chapter. In terms of the world in which the child lives, this principle means that he will tend to adopt the patterns of behavior that are prominently engaged in by his family, his classmates, the neighborhood gang, and other groups of children and adults with whom he associates.

(7) *The power of the model to induce actual performance (as distinguished from acquisition) is strongly influenced by the observed consequences for the model of the exhibited behavior.* If the model's actions bring about pleasurable or attractive outcomes, then the child is more likely to perform the observed behavior. In contrast, punishment for the model's behavior leads to an inhibition of the observed performance on the part of the child.[39]

For example, in one Bandura experiment, children observed models performing aggressively (striking a toy doll) and then receiving either reward or punishment for this act.[40] As a result, the children imitated the aggression of the rewarded model—but not of the model who had been punished. Later, however, when the children who had observed the punished model were led to believe they would be rewarded for aggression, they displayed the aggressive behavior. Both groups of children had thus *acquired* the aggressive behavior but the model-punished group did not *perform* what they had learned until they could anticipate positive consequences.

We note in this principle an interaction between effects of modeling and those of social reinforcement, the topic with which we next concern ourselves.

Social Reinforcement

As we have seen, other people can influence the child by serving not only as models but as reinforcing agents; that is, by giving affection, approval, or providing some other gratifying experience when the child exhibits the desired behavior (even if only in crude form), it is possible to increase the frequency and precision of that behavior on the part of the child. Conversely, punishing or disapproving some form of behavior decreases its occurrence. In recent years psychological research has revealed that the range and variety of stimuli which can serve as reinforcers for a child extend well beyond conventional conceptions of reward or punishment. For example, investigators have demonstrated that vocalization in infants can be significantly increased by such seemingly inconsequential acts as a smile, a touch of the hand, a movement of the head, or a barely audible clucking noise.[41] It is significant that these are precisely the ways in which mothers, and other persons dealing with young children, have responded from time immemorial to spontaneous activities on the part of their charges, *provided the situation permitted dealing with the child on a one-to-one basis thus permitting frequent selective responses on the part of a reinforcing agent.*

As in the case of modeling, the potency of reinforcement is increased as a function of the child's emotional attachment to the person giving the reinforcement, so that once again the child's parents, friends, and intimate associates emerge, at least potentially, as the most important agents for motivating the child's behavior and development. And again as in the case of modeling, the potency of the reinforcing agent increases with the extent to which he is perceived as having high status and control over resources.[42]

But it is where reinforcement can be combined with modeling that it can have its maximal impact. One way of exploiting this joint effect is to employ reinforcing stimuli which simultaneously serve as models of the behavior to be learned. Thus one of the most efficient procedures for developing the young child's capacity for communication is to respond to his spontaneous utterances with ordinary conversation at gradually increasing levels of complexity.

In the preceding example, the model and the reinforcer are the same person. But once a child becomes conscious of his social world, still another advantageous mix of these two strategies becomes possible. This is the technique of so-called *vicarious reinforcement* in which the person reinforced is not the learner (i.e., the child) but the model. As we have already seen, rewarding the model for exhibiting a particular behavior pattern increases the frequency of that behavior in a child observing the model. In addition, the reinforcing power of the model is also enhanced. In other words, if we wish to maximize the development of a particular skill or behavior in the child we do well to reinforce not only the child himself, but also the models manifesting the desired behavior, who in turn would also reinforce the child. Note that this optimal arrangement requires the involvement of at least three persons—the child himself, a model, and a reinforcer. It is of course precisely this kind of triad that is found in the human family, but it can also be introduced into any group structure of more than three persons, such as a classroom, work team, etc. We see here an illustration of the special leverage available in a group for producing behavior change, a topic to which we shall return shortly. But first we must take note of a possible problem in the use of reinforcement as a technique for facilitating learning.

Effective reinforcement requires discrimination on the part of the reinforcer. His response must be contingent upon manifestation of the desired behavior on the part of the child. If he rewards the "wrong behavior" or if he simply provides general- ized gratification unrelated to particular activities of the child, there will be no increase in the desired behavior. This lack of appropriately discriminating response presents a problem in the everyday world of the disadvantaged child. In that world, par- ents and other potential reinforcing agents are so harassed and distracted that they are often unable to pay much attention to their children.[43] It is all these parents can do to keep their chil- dren alive, to get them clothed, fed, housed, and free of disease. Under the pressures of a deprived and threatening environ- ment, there is neither time nor temper for playing games with children, answering their questions, or praising their construc- tive efforts. To the extent that the child gets any attention at all in response to his own activity, it is likely to be when he misbe- haves to the point of interfering with the adults. Thus, in con- trast to the middle-class youngster, who is reinforced for curios- ity and achievement, the disadvantaged child grows up in a world of few contingent responses that would lead him to see the probability of reward arising out of his own efforts. Instead, what little he learns about the connection between his own be- havior and its social consequence is counterproductive for the development of the motives and skills required for satisfactory progress in the worlds of school and work.

It is probably through such counterproductive experiences such as these that the child develops a feeling of inability to affect or change his environment.[44] That such feelings can in- fluence academic achievement has been documented by many investigators,[45] and is particularly evident in the findings of the Coleman report. Thus in the light of his data, Coleman specu- lates:

> . . . Having experienced an unresponsive environment, the virtues of hard work, of diligent and extended effort to- ward achievement appear to such a [disadvantaged] child unlikely to be rewarding. As a consequence, he is likely to merely "adjust" to his environment, finding satisfaction in passive pursuits. It may well be, then, that one of the keys toward success for minorities which have experienced dis-

advantage and a particularly unresponsive environment—either in the home or the larger society—is a change in this conception.[46]

What social reinforcement such a child does receive in school is likely to be more contingent upon his *label* as "disadvantaged" than upon his actual behavior. A concrete illustration of this process is useful because it highlights both a mistaken attribution of "cause" and subsequent inappropriate action which stem from this attribution. Let us consider a teacher who sees that two of her pupils are doing poorly and seeks an explanation. In her records, one of these children, Don, is labeled "disadvantaged," while the other, Albert, comes from a middle-class home. In the case of Don, she can easily *attribute* the cause of his poor performance to *him* because he has been "deprived" and cannot be expected to perform well. For Albert, however, she has no such ready explanation and hence may attribute the cause of his poor performance to *her* failure. As a result, she begins to react to the two boys quite differently. Albert receives more attention; Don less, since the "reasons" for his failure are "beyond her control." In due course, Albert's performance improves, while Don's deteriorates—thus validating the prior judgment of both teacher and school.

This subtle process of mistaken attribution and its consequences has been termed "the Rosenthal effect" after the social psychologist who first demonstrated its impact systematically.[47] In Robert Rosenthal's experiments, teachers were informed that certain of their pupils could be expected to improve their academic performance substantially during the year. These children, labeled "spurters," were in fact chosen at random. The results revealed that children from whom the teachers were led to expect gains, did in fact show marked improvement, in comparison to matched controls, on objective tests of ability. The largest increments were found in the first and second grades, where the average gains in IQ were 27 and 16 points respectively.

Although the nature of the process underlying the Rosenthal effect is not yet clear, there can be no doubt that social reinforcement is heavily involved. Moreover, once the process can be understood and consciously controlled, it carries major implications for educational practice. In Rosenthal's words:

> If it could be learned how [the teacher] is able to bring about dramatic improvement in the performance of her pupils without formal changes in her methods of teaching, other teachers could be taught to do the same. If further research showed that it is possible to find teachers whose untrained educational style does for their pupils what our teachers did for the special children, the prospect would arise that a combination of sophisticated selection of teachers and suitable training of teachers would give all children a boost toward getting as much as they possibly can out of their schooling.[48]

Intensive Relationships

In our discussion both of modeling and reinforcement we noted that the most potent agents for each of these processes were persons with whom the child has developed intensive and enduring relationships; typically his parents, relatives, and other persons, both children and adults, with whom he becomes closely involved on a day-to-day basis. We consider next some evidence bearing on this issue and its implications for the socialization process.

There is substantial body of data demonstrating the powerful effect of parents as models in shaping the behavior and psychological development of the child.[49] The evidence is as eloquent in negative as in positive instances. For example, the difficulties of the disadvantaged child upon entry into school have been traced by a number of investigators to lack of stimulation, both cognitive and motivational, in his home environment.[50] But, at the same time, other studies show that where conditions permit forming and maintaining an intensive relationship with the child, even a presumably inadequate mother can do a great deal for the development of a seriously deprived child. The most dramatic evidence on this score comes from

Harold Skeels' remarkable follow-up study of two groups of mentally retarded, institutionalized children, who constituted the experimental and control groups in an experiment he had initiated thirty years earlier.[51] When the children were three years of age, 13 of them were placed in the care of female inmates of a state institution for the mentally retarded, with each child being assigned to a different ward.

A control group was allowed to remain in the original—also institutional—environment, a children's orphanage. During the formal experimental period, which averaged a year and a half, the experimental group showed a gain in IQ of 28 points (from 64 to 92), whereas the control group dropped 26 points. Upon completion of the experiment, it became possible to place the institutionally-mothered children in legal adoption. Thirty years later, all 13 children in the experimental group were found to be self-supporting, all but two had completed high school, with four having one or more years of college. In the control group, all were either dead or still institutionalized.

Other studies, less dramatic but with larger samples, point to similar conclusions; these findings have already been summarized by Bronfenbrenner.[52] Most of them deal with the focal role of the mother or mother substitute, but we have also noted the debilitating effects of father absence on the psychological development of children, especially boys (see pages 71–72, 104). Regrettably, little work has been done on the specific influence on the child of other family members or intimate associates— such as a sibling, grandparents, close friends, or older children and adults. But there is every reason to expect that their potency as models or reinforcers will be a direct function of the intensity of the child's association and emotional involvement with them.

The foregoing discussion carries a number of provocative implications for educational and social programs. To begin with, it suggests that insuring a high level of expertise in the persons dealing directly with the child may not be as critical for furthering the child's psychological development as creating possibilities for those who are potentially the most powerful influences in the child's life, his parents, friends, and immediate associates, to realize their potential.

Putting the issue in this way makes clear that the matter is not so simple. Some level of "expertise" on the part of the "teacher" is obviously essential if the child is to learn the skills, behaviors, and motives necessary to cope successfully with his environment. It is precisely these skills, behaviors, and motives that must be exhibited in the behavior of the persons surrounding the child and be reinforced by them. But, as we have already seen, this is precisely what does not happen in the day-to-day world of the disadvantaged child. His parents and other intimate associates often do not exhibit an adequately high level of the behavior and motives which the child most needs to learn. Nor do they sufficiently often reinforce such behaviors when they are exhibited by the child or by others in his environment. Such attention as is given is not appropriately discriminating. Often it is so generalized and diffuse as to have no impact in selective reinforcement; on other occasions it is differentially responsive not to the expressions of the child's constructive capacities, but his passive reactions or disruptive behavior.

This brings us to an important question. Is the problem that persons in the day-to-day environment of the disadvantaged child *cannot* engage in behavior appropriate to his needs because they lack the requisite ability or skill? Or are they capable of such behavior, but simply do not engage in it because they are not motivated to do so?

Undoubtedly both considerations play a part, but the available evidence suggests that the second factor is more important than the first. For example, we read in Skeels' account that the mentally-retarded "mothers" in the institution "spent a great deal of time with 'their children,' playing, talking, and training them in every way. The children received constant attention and were the recipients of gifts; they were taken on excursions and were exposed to special opportunities of all kinds." Nor were the mothers themselves without models and reinforcers, for the ward attendants also spent "a great deal of time" with the children, and the matron in charge introduced "new play materials, additional language stimulation," and other special experiences.

In other words, given motivation, opportunity, and exposure to the kinds of activities that are enjoyable and instructive for young children, parents and other close associates of children from disadvantaged backgrounds can do a great deal to further the psychological development of the child in their midst.

There is a second and even more compelling reason for actively involving parents and other persons close to the child in the compensatory program. We have noted that models are influential not only in instigating new behavior patterns but also in determining which patterns already in the child's repertoire are activated and maintained and which are allowed to be extinguished. As the most powerful models for the child, parents and other intimate associates thus become not only the most important potential agents for bringing about change in the child's behavior, but also the principal figures who maintain established patterns of activity (whether adaptive or non-adaptive), and who, insofar as they fail to expose the child to constructive experiences, prevent him from realizing his full potential. In short, it is the parents and other close companions of the child who are the primary determiners not only of what the child learns, but what he fails to learn.

It follows that any appreciable, enduring improvement in the child's development can be effected only through an appreciable, enduring change in the environment and behavior of the persons intimately associated with the child on a day-to-day basis.

Given our analysis of contemporary trends in the lives of America's children, it is possible to go one step further and indicate the nature of the changes that need to be brought about. For the society as a whole, forces must be set in motion which will lead to greater involvement of adults in the lives of children. For the disadvantaged families of the society, this means, first of all, providing relief from the overwhelming burden of sheer survival. No parent who spends his days in search of menial work, and his nights in keeping rats away from the crib, can be expected to find the time—let alone the heart—to serve as an inspiring model for his children or as a stable source of support and control. Only when the basic needs are met can we turn to the next level of providing opportunities for parents, adults, and older children to learn new skills and satisfactions in working with the young. Moreover, such opportunities must be provided in a way which will not deprive the learner of his self-respect and sense of human dignity. To do so, we must design programs that educate and motivate people while not demeaning and humiliating them.

How can such a radical change be brought about? For answers to this question, we consider still another social context in which the processes of modeling and reinforcement can thrive, namely, a structure extending beyond an intensive relationship between two people to include a number of persons sharing a sense of common identity in a *group*.

Group Forces

The power of group forces in shaping the behavior of the child has already been documented in connection with our earlier discussion of peer groups (*pages 101–109*). We have also seen how the potency of modeling and reinforcement are enhanced when they occur in the context of a group of which the child is or aspires to be a member. In particular, we have noted the decisive influence of the classroom group on the child's academic achievement. This phenomenon provides a striking illustration of the power of the group to modify the behavior of its members. Even though each classmate taken alone presents an incomplete model of the behavior to be learned and is a less-skilled and less-motivated instructor than the teacher, the cumulative beneficial effect of being in a classroom with able, motivated pupils is substantially greater than what can be achieved by a single teacher. This result comes about not only because other class members serve as models and reinforcers of good performance, but also because the child's dependence on the group, his desire to belong, serves as an additional motivating factor to behave like the others. Nor is the classroom the only group to which the child belongs or is attracted. Neighborhood gangs, play groups, social groups, etc., make up an important and largely untapped source of influence in the everyday life of the child.

How can they be used to constructive advantage? Let us consider an example much talked about in connection with compensatory programs for children in preschool and primary grades: namely, the use of teen-agers from the neighborhood as tutors, escorts, and play supervisors. Much in the manner of the inmate mothers in the Skeels experiment, the neighborhood youths can function as models and reinforcers for the young. In terms of the principles we have outlined, older children are well suited to the task. They are certainly more similar to their charges than middle-class adolescents or adults; they are likely to be perceived as powerful and admired figures by their young charges; they represent groups which the children look up to.

But there is a problem. Although teen-agers from disadvantaged backgrounds exhibit some behavior (e.g., use of words in sentences) which the deprived child needs to learn, much might also be learned that would be negative in its impact, not only in the cognitive but even more in the emotional and social spheres. Similar considerations apply to the other actual and potential models from the day-to-day world of the disadvantaged child. The amount of assimilable, competent, or constructive behavior which they typically exhibit may be far too small, and heavily outweighed by non-constructive or even negative elements.

Fortunately, what is typical is not thereby inevitable. In the case of older children and adults, where some competence and capacity for constructive action already exist within the behavioral repertoire, it is possible to increase substantially the amount of such behavior that is actually exhibited by structuring the social situation so that it invites and requires such behavior. Contemporary research suggests that such a change can be accomplished by utilizing the motivating power of what Muzafer Sherif has called "superordinate goals."[53]

Superordinate Goals

In the early nineteen-fifties, Sherif and his colleagues at the University of Oklahoma conducted a study known as the "Robbers Cave Experiment."[54] In the words of Elton B. McNeil:

> War was declared at Robbers Cave, Oklahoma, in the summer of 1954. . . .[55] Of course, if you have seen one war you have seen them all, but this was an interesting war, as wars go, because only the observers knew what the fighting was about. How, then, did this war differ from any other war? This one was caused, conducted, and concluded by behavioral scientists. After years of religious, political, and economic wars, this was, perhaps, the first scientific war. It wasn't the kind of war that an adventurer could join just for the thrill of it. To be eligible, ideally, you had to be an eleven-year-old, middle-class, American, Protestant, well-adjusted boy who was willing to go to an experimental camp.[56]

Sherif set out to demonstrate that, within the space of a few weeks, he could bring about two sharply contrasting patterns of behavior in this sample of normal boys. First, he would transform them into hostile, destructive, antisocial gangs; then, within a few days, change them into cooperative, constructive workers and friends concerned about and even ready to make sacrifices for other members of the community.

The success of the effort can be gauged by the following two excerpts describing the behavior of the boys after each stage had been reached. After the first "experimental treatment" was introduced,

> . . . good feeling soon evaporated. The members of each group began to call their rivals "stinkers," "sneaks," and "cheaters." They refused to have anything more to do with individuals in the opposing group. The boys . . . turned against buddies whom they had chosen as "best friends" when they first arrived at the camp. A large proportion of the boys in each group gave negative ratings to all the boys in the other. The rival groups made threatening posters

and planned raids, collecting secret hoards of green apples for ammunition. In the Robbers Cave camp, the Eagles, after a defeat in a tournament game, burned a banner left behind by the Rattlers; the next morning the Rattlers seized the Eagles' flag when they arrived on the athletic field. From that time on name-calling, scuffles and raids were the rule of the day. . . . In the dining-hall line they shoved each other aside, and the group that lost the contest for the head of the line shouted "Ladies first!" at the winner. They threw paper, food and vile names at each other at the tables. An Eagle bumped by a Rattler was admonished by his fellow Eagles to brush "the dirt" off his clothes.

But after the second experimental treatment,

. . . The members of the two groups began to feel more friendly to each other. For example, a Rattler whom the Eagles disliked for his sharp tongue and skill in defeating them became a "good egg." The boys stopped shoving in the meal line. They no longer called each other names, and sat together at the table. New friendships developed between individuals in the two groups.

In the end the groups were actively seeking opportunities to mingle, to entertain and "treat" each other. They decided to hold a joint campfire. They took turns presenting skits and songs. Members of both groups requested that they go home together on the same bus, rather than on the separate buses in which they had come. On the way the bus stopped for refreshments. One group still had five dollars which they had won as a prize in a contest. They decided to spend this sum on refreshments. On their own initiative they invited their former rivals to be their guests for malted milks.

How was each of these effects achieved? Treatment One has a familiar ring:

. . . To produce friction between the groups of boys we arranged a tournament of games: baseball, touch football, a tug-of-war, a treasure hunt and so on. The tournament started in a spirit of good sportsmanship. But as it progressed good feeling soon evaporated.

The dynamics of the process are best described in the words of a sportswriter acquaintance: "Sherif," he said, "was just applying the Vince Lombardi ethic." He then quoted the classical statement by the coach of the world-champion Green Bay Packers: "Winning isn't everything; it's the *only* thing!"

But how does one turn hatred into harmony? Before undertaking this task, Sherif wanted to demonstrate that, contrary to the views of some students of human conflict, mere interaction —pleasant social contact between antagonists—would not reduce hostility.

> . . . we brought the hostile Rattlers and Eagles together for social events: going to the movies, eating in the same dining room and so on. But far from reducing conflict, these situations only served as opportunities for the rival groups to berate and attack each other.

How was conflict finally dispelled? By a series of stratagems, of which the following is an example.

> . . . Water came to our camp in pipes from a tank about a mile away. We arranged to interrupt it and then called the boys together to inform them of the crisis. Both groups promptly volunteered to search the water line for trouble. They worked together harmoniously, and before the end of the afternoon they had located and corrected the difficulty.[57]

On another occasion, just when everyone was hungry and the camp truck was about to go to town for food, it developed that the engine wouldn't start, and the boys had to pull together to get the vehicle going.

To move from practice to principle, according to Sherif, the critical element for achieving harmony in human relations is joint activity in behalf of a *superordinate goal*. "Hostility gives way when groups pull together to achieve overriding goals which are real and compelling for all concerned."

An example in a different setting comes from a Head Start Program operating in an urban slum. The problem was getting children to and from the center in a "tough neighborhood." Since not enough parents were available at the needed hours, the staff turned for help to the local gang, the "Golden Bombers." The resulting operation was a sight to behold as twice every day the Bombers, in "snap formation" proudly conducted their charges through heavy traffic with "complete protection." What is more, after seeing what was going on at the center, they volunteered to help by reading to the children, taking them on outings, etc.

What the Bombers did, of course, was to adopt the care of this Head Start group as a "goal of the gang." They were able to do so even through it was not part of their original motive in forming the gang—the original motive, as in many youth gangs in ghetto areas, was reportedly "self-protection."

The power of superordinate goals in mobilizing constructive group activities is also reflected in the success of Skeels' experiment. It was not only the intensive relationship between the child and his mentally retarded "mother" that is to be credited for bringing about the striking changes that occurred. As Skeels takes pains to point out, with the appearance of a young child needing care, not only each ward, including inmates, attendants, and head matron, but the institution as a whole became involved in the enterprise; e.g., "There was considerable competition among wards to see which one would have its 'baby' walking or talking first."

Indeed, we can now recognize that Skeels' experimental treatment involved all of the elements we have discussed as especially potent for facilitating constructive behavior and development in children; that is, the modeling and reinforcement made possible by an enduring intensive relationship are enhanced by group commitment to a common superordinate goal —such as caring for a little child.

It is the utilization of precisely this same superordinate goal which, in our view, offers the greatest promise for the design of effective educational and social programs. In our discussion up to this point we have repeatedly been confronted with the same problem: how to "turn off" the predominantly negative and counterproductive behavior often exhibited by the most significant persons in the life of the child and to evoke, in its place, constructive behavior of which these persons are actually capable. We now see that superordinate goals have the power of effecting precisely this kind of behavior change. Specifically, involving persons actually or potentially important to the child in pursuit of a superordinate goal can have the effect of maximizing the incidence and inductive power of constructive behaviors and motives while reducing disruptive and negative influences.

But the mere acceptance of a superordinate goal will not necessarily lead to effective, cooperative action. A second important element is the institution of what might be called "common paths"; that is, the various groups or individuals involved in the pursuit of a given superordinate goal must agree upon the method of attaining that goal and the roles they will play. It is both the shared objective and the mutually-agreed-upon manner of achieving this objective that produce results.

Achieving such consensus on ends and means calls for a high level of cooperation between the various individuals and groups involved. To the extent that this ideal is not achieved, then the outcomes for the child are less sure. Aside from the energy wasted in duplication, it may often occur that the different programs work at counterpurposes. More often than not, these counterproductive results are unnecessary; the differences between the apparently divergent groups are often matters of rhetoric and not practice, and the conflicts can be resolved in the name of a superordinate goal to which all parties are at root committed.

But is it possible to find a particular superordinate goal that would have appeal across such demonstrably divisive barriers as age, class, and color? We believe that such a common, potentially-strongly-motivating concern exists. That concern is the young child of poverty, whose need for help speaks out eloquently to all who see him. In other words, we are proposing that, if we turn to any existing or potential segment of this child's world, be it his immediate family, his actual or possible classmates, older children or adults from his own neighborhood or from the other side of the tracks, and ask their cooperation in activities in behalf of the child, such cooperation will be given competently and conscientiously, provided that the nature of the requisite activity is clear and lies within the capability of the individual or group of whom it is requested.

Nor is service to the very young the only superordinate goal relevant to children in our society. There are also the very old. In segregating them in their own housing projects and, indeed, in whole communities, we have deprived both them and the younger generation of an essential human experience. We need to find ways in which children can once again have contact with old people, to assist and comfort them, and, in return, gain the benefits to character development which accrue from these experiences. For it is not only the disadvantaged or the old who gain from such humane actions. Although contemporary American middle-class society and its children are not suffering effects of cognitive deprivation, they are by no means free from a variety of social and emotional ills, prominent among which are problems of apathy, alienation, and antisocial behavior; and it is participation in service to others that provides the most promising antidote for these social maladies. Thus the constructive effects of such cooperative endeavors are reflected not only in the lives of those who are its target, but of those who engage in the effort—the "have's" no less than the "have not's."

Soviet Upbringing Revisited

We have now completed our examination of the major environmental forces and conditions which can influence the behavior and development of children. With this perspective, it is instructive to look back briefly at Soviet methods of upbringing, and to reconsider them in the light of the principles of intervention we have formulated. To do so is to become aware how thoroughly these principles have been exploited in Soviet educational practice. The concern for the nutrition and health of infants and pregnant mothers, the heavy use of modeling through the large-scale involvement of older children and adults in work with younger age groups, the deliberate employment of

group forces in reinforcing desired behaviors within the enduring social context of the collective, and the assignment of responsibilities even to the very young in the name of superordinate goals in the classroom, the school, and the community*
—all of these qualify as examples *par excellence* of the strategies we have laid out as representing our most powerful resources for influencing the socialization process.

Yet virtually all of the research used as the basis for deriving our principles was done in the West. Social psychology did not begin to be regarded as a legitimate discipline in the Soviet Union until the late nineteen-fifties (reviewed by Bronfenbrenner),[58] and systematic experimental studies have only recently begun to appear (such as M. S. Neimark's).[59] Thus we are confronted with a paradox: the principles that we in the West have investigated in—and largely confined to—the laboratory, the Russians have discovered and applied in practice on a national scale. Yet these principles belong to science, not only to the Soviets. Having been derived from Western research, they should certainly be applicable to Western society and its institutions. It is this possibility which we explore in our final chapter.

* A Soviet formulation of the concept of superordinate goals and its importance in the socialization of a child is found in the following statement by Novikova: "The children's collective cannot develop, cannot move forward unless there stands before it a common goal which all the members accept as a vitally important aspiration, for the sake of which they enter into relations with one another, unite their efforts, and overcome difficulties." From "Vospitanie lichnosti v kollektive [The Development of Personality in the Collective]," *Sovetskaya pedagogika* [*Soviet Pedagogy*], XXXI, No. 3 (1967), 111.

6

From Science to Social Action

WE NOW CONSIDER how the principles we have derived from research can be applied within the framework of the major American institutions involved in the process of socialization. Clearly the institution which stands at the core of the process in our own culture is the family. And it is the withdrawal of the family from its child-rearing functions that we have identified as a major factor threatening the breakdown of the socialization process in America. Yet, it is not with the family that we propose to begin our discussion of how the needs of children can be most effectively served. Instead we consider first innovations in our educational institutions—specifically classrooms and schools.

The reason for this reversal springs from our social psychological perspective and the picture it reveals of the sources of resistance and change in a social system. In particular, our analysis points to a paradoxical situation. Even though the lack of parental involvement lies at the heart of our present malaise, parents by themselves can do little to bring about the needed change. For, as we have seen, it is not primarily the family, but other institutions in our society that determine how and with whom children spend their time, and it is these institutions that have created and perpetuate the age-segregated, and thereby often amoral or antisocial, world in which our children live and grow. Central among the institutions which, by their structure and limited concern, have encouraged these socially disruptive developments have been our schools. Accordingly, it is with these that we begin our exploration of possibilities for innovation.

In all, we shall consider changes in five major contexts affecting the lives of children: the Classroom, the School, the Family, the Neighborhood, and the Larger Community.

The Classroom

In terms of human potential, the classroom contains two major sources for influencing behavior and development: the teacher, and the children themselves.

POTENTIALITIES IN THE TEACHER'S ROLE

In keeping with the traditional emphasis of American schools on conveying subject matter, the teacher has been perceived and has functioned primarily in the role of resource person and giver of information. It is this emphasis which is reflected in Western research on teaching, as documented by N. L. Gage.[1] Only recently has the work of Rosenthal (*see page 138*) called attention to the powerful impact of the teacher as a reinforcer (often unrecognized by herself), whereas her potency as a model is yet to be examined through systematic research.

But social processes do not wait in the wings for their appearance to be ratified by the data of behavioral science. They function notwithstanding, and their unintended consequences can often be counterproductive. A case in point is provided by the vicious circle set in motion by a teacher's labeling of a child as "disadvantaged" (*see pages 138–139*) or her tendency to give problem pupils individualized attention—that is, reinforcement—primarily when they display disruptive behavior.[2]

The greatest promise for constructive change, however, lies not with errors of commission but of omission—the failure to provide and reinforce models of desired behavior. We have in mind here not so much the failure of the teacher to set a good example (although, as we shall indicate, much more can be accomplished along these lines), but rather the absence in the classroom and its activities of other models besides the teacher and the children themselves. We view the introduction of such models as desirable, feasible, and central to the teacher's task.

In other words, our discussion implies a broadened conception of the teacher's role. Not only must she herself function as a motivating model, but *it becomes her responsibility to seek out, organize, develop, and coordinate the activities of other appropriate models and reinforcing agents both within the classroom and outside.* How this might be done will become apparent as we proceed.

For the teacher herself to function as an effective model and reinforcer, she must possess the characteristics which we have identified as enhancing inductive power; that is, she must be perceived by the pupils as a person of status who has control over resources. In our view, it is to the advantage of the educational process, and thus to the entire society, to insure that this is, in fact, the case. Teachers who are poorly paid, treated as subordinates, and given little freedom and autonomy by the school administration cannot help but reflect their true position and reduce their influence in the pupil's eyes. A person must have a measure of self-respect and status before he can expect others to admire these traits in him. The occasional teacher who would exploit such power is less of a risk than the devastating loss of good teachers whose functioning is impaired due to the constraints in the present system. When teachers have a true stake in the development of the children under their care, when they have the responsibility and autonomy so often admired and seldom granted, then they themselves can be expected to bring social pressure on the occasional deviant colleague who might abuse this freedom, or, more importantly, on those who fail to use their freedom to act as the agents of society in the forming of the next generation. Moreover, in that task, the teacher must reflect not the preferences and prejudices of a particular class, but the interests of all segments of the society in their quest for a better world.

Finally, if the above considerations are accepted as valid, they call for radical changes in our current practices of teacher-selection and -training. Specifically, they argue for the recruitment of persons on other than purely academic qualifications, with at least as much emphasis placed on social as on intellectual qualities and skills. For example, the research evidence indicates that learning is facilitated when the teacher is similar to the child in cultural background, race, and, especially in the case of boys, sex. Such findings argue for the recruitment of many more persons from disadvantaged and minority groups—especially males—into the teaching profession and other occupations involving work with young children. But it is in the realm of teacher-training that the most far-reaching innovations are required. In addition to knowing his subject, the teacher of tomorrow must acquire both understanding and skill in the use of modeling, social reinforcement, and group processes in work with children. But beyond that, he must know how to discover, recruit, and utilize individuals and groups from outside the school as major adjuncts to the educational process. This implies a far better acquaintance and articulation with the local community—its people, problems, and resources—than has ever been required or expected of teachers in the past.

But before we examine the extension of the teaching process outside the school, we need to consider further potentials for innovation within the classroom itself.

POTENTIALITIES OF THE CLASSROOM GROUP

This is one of the most promising and least exploited areas for effecting behavioral change. Although modifications of classroom composition in terms of social class and race can have salutary effects, they by no means represent the most powerful resources at our disposal. Indeed, their potential is realized only to the extent that they facilitate development of the motivating processes (modeling, reinforcement, group commitment, involvement in superordinate goals, etc.) we have outlined. Such development need not be left to chance. It can be directly fostered through setting up within the classroom the kinds of social and situational structures in which these processes thrive. This includes such devices as teams, cooperative group competition, organized patterns of mutual help, etc., including the incorporation into such social units of different mixes of race, social class, sex, achievement level, and the like. In short, we must learn to make more effective use of group forces in fostering human development. As we have seen, the power of the group, including the children's group, in motivating goal-directed activity in its members is well established in American social science, but the practical implications of this knowledge for education have thus far remained unexploited in this country. Where practical applications have been made on a broad scale, as in the Soviet Union, the programs have not yet been subjected to systematic empirical analysis and evaluation. It remains for American educators and social scientists to apply the findings of research in the design of educational experiments susceptible to rigorous test and to the improvements which such evaluation makes possible. For example, one might start by examining the effectiveness of two-pupil teams composed of children of heterogeneous ability designated as partners or playmates, and compare their progress with unpaired individuals or members of homogeneous pairs. Another possibility draws on the potency of group reinforcement by introducing such "customs" as group applause for correct answers, selection and honoring by classmates of members showing greatest individual progress, etc. *But, surely, the most needed innovation in the American classroom is the involvement of pupils in responsible tasks on behalf of others within the classroom, the school, the neighborhood, and the community.* The full potential of the motivational processes here discussed will remain unplumbed and seriously underestimated so long as the social setting in which these processes can take place is limited to the conventional classroom with its homogeneous grouping, by age, and, often, by ability and social class as well. To realize these possibilities requires moving beyond the classroom into the larger contexts of school and neighborhood.

The School

Perhaps the most promising possibility which the total school offers in furthering the development of the child is the active involvement of older and, subsequently, younger children in the process. For the preschooler or primary-grader, an older child, particularly of the same sex, can be a very influential figure, especially if he is willing to spend time with his younger companion. Except for the occasional anachronism of a one-room school, this potential resource remains almost entirely unexploited in American education and, for that matter, in the process of socialization generally as it takes place in our country. Opportunities for experimentation are therefore legion. One might begin with an Americanized adaptation of the Soviet system of *"shevstvo"* in which a preschool or primary class is "adopted" by an older class, with each younger child having an older "brother" or "sister" from the more advanced class. It becomes the responsibility of the older pupil to get to know his younger "sib" and his family, to escort him to and from school, play with him and his friends, teach him games, and, last but not least, become acquainted with his progress and problems in school, reading with and to him, helping and encouraging him to learn. In the meantime the parent class as a whole organizes activities for their "ward class," including trips to athletic events, nature walks, camp-outs, museum visits, etc.

The foregoing examples illustrate how an enduring social situation can be created that simultaneously exploits all of the motivating processes and social structures outlined earlier, for here the effects of modeling and reinforcement are enhanced in the context of intensive relationships, group membership, and common commitment to a superordinate goal.

An extension of this same principle points to a potential contribution of the school as a whole to the development of the individual child. Within the formal educational context, the school is the social unit with which the child, and those concerned for his welfare, can most readily identify. If the school as a total community becomes visibly involved in activities focused on the child and his needs, if older children, school organizations, other teachers, school administrators, PTA's—if all these persons and groups in some way participate in the program and publicly support those most actively engaged in the effort, the reinforcing effect increases by geometric proportions. Conversely, if a special program is confined to an isolated class-room, it is not only deprived of powerful reinforcing influences but also risks the danger that the rest of the school, especially children in other classes, will perceive the "special class" in invidious terms (e.g., "dummies, queers") and treat its members accordingly. When this occurs, the powerful influences of modeling, negative reinforcement, and group pressure serve only to undermine the already unfavorable self-image of a "problem child."

But it is not primarily the needs of problem children or the disadvantaged that call for change in American schools. If the radical innovations that are required are not introduced, it will be *all* children who will be culturally deprived—not of cognitive stimulation, but of their humanity. For their own full development, the young need to be exposed not only to factual knowledge but also to the standards and modes of behavior requisite for living in a cooperative society. As we have seen, in Communist schools, a deliberate effort is made—through appropriate models, reinforcements, and group experiences—to teach the child the values and *behaviors* consistent with Communist ideals. In American schools, training for action consistent with social responsibility and human dignity is at best an extracurricular activity. The belated recognition of our full educational obligations to the nation's children—the so-called advantaged no less than the deprived—offers us a chance to redress this weakness and to make democratic education not only a principle but a practice.

The Family

Just as a chain breaks first in its weakest link, so the problems of a society become most pressing and visible in the social strata that are under greatest stress. Thus, it is not surprising that we should first recognize the disruption of the process of socialization in American society among the families of the poor. And it is in this same context that we have begun the attempt to develop countermeasures, ways to revitalize the socialization process through the establishment of institutions like Head Start, which re-involve parents and other community members in the lives of their children in a setting that points the way to more constructive patterns of activity and interaction.

Accordingly, in discussing new patterns of family involvement, we draw heavily on the experience of the author as a member of the committee that originally designed and gave professional direction to the Head Start program. Although most of our examples refer to the disadvantaged family, they are readily translatable into the middle-class world, as evidenced by the increasing demand for—and inception of—Head Start–type programs in well-to-do neighborhoods.

Today's Head Start programs typically profess strong commitment to the principle of family involvement, but in practice implementation is limited to two rather restricted forms: the first is the inclusion of some parents on the program's advisory board; the second involves meetings for parents at which staff members make presentations about some aspect of the program. Both of these measures have the effect of bypassing the most important aspect of family involvement—engaging parents and older children in new and more mutually rewarding patterns of interaction with the young.

An essential first step in bringing about such changed patterns of interaction is exposure of the parents and other family members to them. This can be done at one of two places, at a preschool or neighborhood center, or in the home. The basic approach is one of demonstration: showing the family the kinds of things that are done in a preschool program, which also happen to be things that family members can themselves do with the child; e.g., games to play, books to read, pictures to look at and talk about. Particularly valuable in this connection are activities that involve and require more than one person in patterns of interaction with the child; that is, not just the teacher and/or the mother, but also other adults and older children (i.e., father, grandma, brother, sister, next-door neighbor). A useful technique is to ask the visiting or visited family members to help in carrying out particular activities with the child. It is important that the process not be seen as a lesson in which the child must learn something and deserves punishment for failure, but instead simply as an engaging activity in which learning is incidental to a total gratifying experience.

To facilitate the involvement of parents in such non-school-like educational activities, it is desirable to provide a library consisting not only of books but also of toys and games which require the verbal participation of adults and older children, and which can be borrowed for extended periods of time for home use.

The involvement of family members in the educational program of course poses a difficult dilemma to professional staff. On the one hand, there is the need to expose parents and other family members to new or different ways of dealing with their children. On the other hand, this must be done in such a way as to enhance, rather than lower, the power and prestige of these persons in the eyes of the child. The second requirement arises from the evidence that the inductive and reinforcing capacity of a model varies directly with the model's status, command over resources, and control of the social environment. An ingenious demonstration of how this dilemma can be resolved was observed at an all-Negro Head Start program in the rural South. Since the local, white-dominated school administration had refused to have anything to do with the program, it was organized by Negro church groups under the leadership of an eighty-six-year-old minister. Several days before classes were to begin, this man invited all the parents and teen-agers to an orientation meeting, a pass-the-dish picnic in a nearby forest area (a forest which he himself had planted years ago with seeds obtained free from the United States Department of Agriculture). After the picnic, the minister offered to take the whole group on a tour of the forest. During the walk he would ask adults and teen-agers to show him interesting plant and animal life which they observed, give names of flowers, trees, and birds, explain how plants grow, what animals feed on, etc. While drawing out much information from the group, he also added considerable material from his own experience. At the end of the walk, he turned to the group with a request: "On Saturday we start our Head Start program. In the afternoon the children need some recreation and the teachers need a rest. Could you folks bring the children here and tell them all the things *you know* that *they don't know* about the forest?"

The turnout on Saturday was impressive, and so was the performance of the "instant experts."

The Neighborhood

The foregoing example illustrates also the reinforcing potential of the other people with whom the child frequently associates and identifies—his neighbors. These persons, particularly the adults and older children who are looked up to and admired by the young, probably stand second only to parents in terms of their power to influence the child's behavior. For this reason it would be important for educational programs to try to exploit this potential in a systematic way. The most direct approach would be to discover from the families and neighborhoods themselves who are the popular and admired individuals and groups, and then to involve them as aides in the program. It may often be the case that the activities in which such individuals or groups normally engage, indeed, the activities for which they are popular, are not those which one would want children to learn or adopt. This fact should receive consideration, but it should hardly be the determining factor, since the behaviors that matter are those that the model exhibits in the presence of the child. It follows that the activities in which such persons engage as aides, volunteers, and the like must be constructive in nature and reinforce other aspects of the program. They may take a variety of forms: supervising and playing games, exhibiting or teaching a hobby or skill (whittling, playing a musical instrument, magic tricks). The significant factor is that the activity be seen by the child as part of and supporting all of the things the child is doing "in school."

A second important use of neighborhood resources involves exposing the child to successful models in his own locality—

persons coming from his own background who are productive members of society: skilled or semiskilled workers, teachers, or government employees. Providing opportunities for such persons to associate with the children (e.g., as escorts, recreation supervisors, part-time aides, or tutors), tell something about their work, and perhaps have the children visit the person at work can help provide a repertoire of possible occupational goals unknown to many children of poverty today. In view of the frequency of father absence among disadvantaged families and the predominance of female personnel in educational programs generally, the involvement of male adults and teen-agers is highly desirable, especially for boys.

If people from the neighborhood are to be drawn into the program, it is obvious that many desirable activities cannot be carried out effectively if they are to be conducted only during school hours or solely in a school classroom. To begin with, if the program is to have enduring impact, it must influence the child's behavior outside of school as much as in school. Second, a school classroom does not lend itself to many of the kinds of informal activities involving parents, other adults, and older children which have been described above.

Accordingly, some kind of *neighborhood center* becomes a highly desirable feature of any comprehensive educational program. Such a center would have to be open after school, on weekends, and during vacations and have some staff members on duty at all times. The center should be represented to the community not merely as a place where children go but rather where all members of the community go in the joint interest of themselves and their children. The neighborhood center might be housed in a school building, but, if so, facilities available should include other than traditional classrooms with fixed seats.

The Larger Community

The contribution of the total community to educational programs is analogous to that of the neighborhood but now with representatives and resources drawn from the larger context. Use can be made both of older children and adults from middle-class backgrounds provided they are not the only "competent" models on the scene, for without the example and support of "his own people" the child's receptivity to what may then be seen as an alien influence is much reduced. It follows that activities by persons or in settings from outside the child's subculture must be heavily interlaced with representatives from his own world who manifestly cooperate in the total effect. This in turn implies close working relationships of mutual respect between workers from within and outside the child's own milieu. Mutual respect is essential in these relationships, not merely for the purpose of maintaining a viable learning atmosphere, but, more importantly, to further the constructive development of the child's own sense of identity and worth as a person and as a member of society.

However, it is not only what the community does for the child that contributes to his development. Of equal if not greater importance is what he does for that community—quite modestly at first, but gradually at increasing levels of responsibility. As we have noted, it is in part the enforced inutility of children in our society that works to produce feelings of alienation, indifference, and antagonism. Learning early in life the skills and rewards of service to one's community brings with it the benefits of a more stable and gratifying self-identity. Indeed, in the last analysis, the child—so long as he remains a child—must receive more from the community than he can give.

From this point of view, the greatest significance of the total community, especially for the disadvantaged child, lies in the fact that many of the problems he faces, and the possibilities for their solution, are rooted in the community as a whole and are therefore beyond the reach of segmental efforts at the level of the neighborhood, the school, or the home. We have in mind such problems as housing, welfare services, medical care, community recreation programs, sanitation, police services, and television programming.

Given this state of affairs, it is a sobering fact that, neither in our communities nor in the nation as a whole, is there a single agency that is charged with the responsibility of assessing and improving the situation of the child in his total environment. As it stands, the needs of children are parcelled out among a hopeless confusion of agencies with diverse objectives, conflicting jurisdictions, and imperfect channels of communication. The school, the health department, the churches, welfare services, youth organizations, the medical profession, libraries, the police, recreation programs—all of these see the children of the community at one time or another, but no one of them is concerned with the total pattern of life for children in the community: where, how, and with whom they spend their waking hours and what may be the impact of these experiences on the development of the child as an individual and as a member of society. An inquiry of this nature would, we believe, reveal some troubling facts which in themselves could generate concerted action. Accordingly, an important aspect of any program at the level of the total community would be the establishment of a "Commission on Children," which would have as its initial charge finding out how, where, and with whom the children of all ages in the community spend their time. The Commission would include among its members representatives of the major institutions in the community that deal with children, but should also draw in businessmen, parents from all social-class levels, as well as the young themselves, teen-agers from diverse segments of the community who can speak from recent experience. The Commission would be expected to report its findings and recommendations to appropriate executive bodies and to the public at large.

Any report of such a Commission is likely to underscore the inescapable fact that many of the problems which beset the lives of children, and the courses of action necessary to combat these problems, lie beyond the power of the local community to control. The design of housing developments, the determination of working hours for industry, the programming policies of television networks, the training of teachers and the new types of personnel needed to work with the young, and, above all, the priorities of state and federal spending—all of these factors which, in the last analysis, determine how a society treats its children, are superimposed on the community from without and require understanding and action at higher levels.

Yet, our emphasis here is on *local initiative and concern*. We believe this is the place to start, for that is where the children are. For only a hard look at the world in which they live—a world we adults have created for them in large part by default —can convince us of the urgency of their plight and the consequences of our inaction. Then perhaps it will come to pass that, in the words of Isaiah, "A little child shall lead them."

We have come a long way in our comparative study of socialization in the Soviet Union and the United States. We began with descriptive facts, considered their implications in the light of data and theory from the social sciences, and ultimately ended with a blueprint for change within our own society. In doing so we take cognizance of a new, as yet unfamiliar, and surely presumptuous role for the scientist dealing with problems of human development. Yet it is a role we believe the social scientist must take. As his colleagues in the physical sciences have learned to do long ago, he must go beyond natural history to recognize and probe as yet unexploited theoretical possibilities and their practical applications. The present volume represents a beginning effort toward this broader objective. We have sought to demonstrate that the behavioral sciences, though admittedly limited in knowledge and theoretical grasp, can, nevertheless, illuminate both the problems of a society and possible directions for their solution. Specifically, we have used a comparative approach to expose similarities and differences in the process of human socialization as it takes place in the two most powerful nations of our time, the Soviet Union and the United States. We believe that the results of this inquiry indicate that the rather different Soviet approach to the upbringing of the young is not without significance for our own problems. If the Russians have gone too far in subjecting the child and his peer group to conformity to a single set of values imposed by the adult society, perhaps we have reached the point of diminishing returns in allowing excessive autonomy and in failing to utilize the constructive potential of the peer group in developing social responsibility and consideration for others. Moving to counteract this tendency does not mean subscribing to Soviet insistence on the primacy of the collective over the individual or adopting their practice of shifting major responsibility for upbringing from the family to public institutions. On the contrary, what is called for is greater involvement of parents, and other adults, in the lives of children, and—conversely—greater involvement of children in responsibility on behalf of their own family, community, and society at large. Given the fragmented character of modern American life—its growing separatism and violence—such an injunction may appear to some as a pipe dream, but it need not be. For just as autonomy and aggression have their roots in the American tradition, so have neighborliness, civic concern, and devotion to the young. It is to these that we must look if we are to rediscover our moral identity as a society and as a nation.

SOURCE
NOTES

Notes to Introduction

1. A. S. Makarenko, *A Book for Parents* [*Kniga dlya roditelei*] (Moscow: Foreign Languages Publishing House, 1954); American edition, *The Collective Family* (New York: Doubleday, 1967), xi–xii.
2. I. A. Kairov (ed.), *Pedagogicheskii slovar* [*Pedagogical dictionary*], 2 vols. (Moscow Izdatelstvo Akademii Pedagogicheskikh Nauk RSFSR, 1960), II, 530.

Notes to Chapter 1

1. E. I. Volkova (ed.), *Roditeli i deti* [*Parents and Children*] (Moscow: The Academy of Pedagogical Sciences, 1961), 15.
2. *Ibid.*, 2.
3. *Ibid.*, 120.
4. *Ibid.*, 126.
5. I. A. Pechernikova, *Vospitanie poslushaniya i trudolyubiya u detei v semye* [*The Development of Obedience and Diligence among Children in the Family*] (Moscow: Prosveshchenie, 1965), 7.
6. *Ibid.*, 54.
7. *Ibid.*, 103.
8. *Ibid.*, 122.
9. *Ibid.*, 123.
10. *Ibid.*, 124–125.

Notes to Chapter 2

1. N. V. Zaluzhskaya (ed.), *Programma vospitania v detskom sadu* [*The Program of Upbringing in the Kindergarten*] (Moscow: Prosveshchenie, 1964), 23–24.
2. *Ibid.*, 24–25.
3. V. A. Sukhomlinsky, *Vospitanie lichnosti v sovetskoi shkole* [*The Upbringing of the Personality in the Soviet School*] (Kiev: Izdatelstvo Radyanska Shkola, 1965).
4. N. I. Boldyrev (ed.), *Programma vospitatelnoi raboty shkoly* [*The Program of the Upbringing Work of the School*] (Moscow: Izdatelstvo Akademii Pedagogicheskikh Nauk RSFSR, 1960).

5. *Ibid.*, 25–29.
6. *Ibid.*, 76–78.
7. A. Kassof, *The Soviet Youth Program* (Cambridge, Mass.: Harvard University Press, 1965; London: Oxford U.P.)
8. A. S. Makarenko, *The Collective Family*, translated by Robert Daglish (New York: Doubleday, Anchor paper edition, 1967).
9. L. I. Novikova, *Sotsialisticheskoe sorevnovanie v shkole* [*Socialist Competition in the Schools*] (Moscow: Gos. Uchebnopedagog, Izd-vo., 1959).
10. See also, N. I. Boldyrev (ed.), *Organizatsia vospitanie shkolnova uchenicheskovo kollektiva* [*The Organization and Upbringing of the School Pupils' Collective*] (Moscow: Izdatelstvo Akademii Pedagogicheskikh Nauk RSFSR, 1959); L. S. Khodakovsky (ed.), *Printsipy organizatsii shkolnovo kollektiva* [*The Principles of Organization of the School Collective*] (Moscow: Prosveshchenie, 1965); T. E. Konnikova, *Organizatsia kollektiva uchashchikhsya v shkole* [*The Organization of the Pupils' Collective in the School*] (Moscow: Izdatelstvo Akademii Pedagogicheskikh Nauk RSFSR, 1957).
11. Novikova, *op. cit.*, 13.
12. *Ibid.*, 49.
13. *Ibid.*, 49.
14. *Ibid.*, 53.
15. *Ibid.*, 53.
16. *Ibid.*, 53.
17. *Ibid.*, 54.
18. *Ibid.*, 57–58.
19. *Ibid.*, 59.
20. *Ibid.*, 59.
21. L. B. Auslender, *Otchevo? pochemu?* [*What for? Why?*] (Moscow: Ministersteva Zdravookhranenia SSR [Ministry of Health of the USSR], 1960).

NOTES TO CHAPTER 3

1. Percival M. Symonds, *The Psychology of Parent-Child Relationships* (New York: Appleton-Century, 1939); David M. Levy, *Maternal Overprotection* (New York: Columbia University Press, 1943).

2. See Wesley C. Becker, "Consequences of Different Kinds of Parental Discipline," in Martin L. Hoffman and Lois Wladis Hoffman, *Review of Child Development Research*, 2 vols. (New York: Russell Sage Foundation; I, 1964; II, 1966), I, 169–208; Urie Bronfenbrenner, "The Changing American Child," *Journal of Social Issues*, XVII, No. 1 (1961), 6–8; Bronfenbrenner, "Soviet Studies of Personality Development and Socialization," in Raymond Bauer (ed.), *Some Views of Soviet Psychology* (Washington, D.C.: American Psychological Association, 1962), 63–86; Bronfenbrenner, "Early Deprivation: A Cross-Species Analysis," in Grant Newton and Seymour Levine (eds.), *Early Experience and Behavior* (Springfield, Ill.: Charles C Thomas, 1968), 627–764; Bettye M. Caldwell, "The Effects of Infant Care," in Hoffman and Hoffman, *op. cit.*, I, 9–88; John A. Clausen, "Family Structure, Socialization and Personality," in Hoffman and Hoffman, *op. cit.*, II, 1–54; Willard W. Hartup, "Dependence and Independence," in Harold W. Stevenson (ed.), *Child Psychology*, 62nd Yearbook of the National Society for the Study of Education (Chicago: University of Chicago Press, 1963), 333–363.

3. Symonds, *op. cit.*, 18.

4. Urie Bronfenbrenner, "The Changing American Child," *Journal of Social Issues*, XVII, No. 1 (1961), 9.

5. George R. Bach, "Father-Fantasies and Father-typing in Father-Separated Children," *Child Development*, XVII (1946), 63–79; Robert R. Sears, Margaret H. Pintler, and Pauline S. Sears, "Effects of Father-Separation on Preschool Children's Doll Play Aggression," *Child Development*, XVII (1946), 219–243; Lois M. Stolz, *Father Relations of War-Born Children* (Palo Alto: Cal.: Stanford University Press, 1954).

6. Erik Gronseth, "The Impact of Father Absence in Sailor Families upon the Personality Structure and Social Adjustment of Adult Sailor Sons," Part I, in N. Anderson (ed.), *Studies of the Family*, 2 vols. (Göttingen, Germany: Vandenhoeck and Ruprecht, 1957), II, 97–114; David B. Lynn and William L. Sawrey, "The Effects of Father-Absence on Norwegian Boys and Girls," *Journal of Abnormal and Social Psychology*, LIX (1959), 258–262; Per O. Tiller, "Father Absence and Personality Development of Children

in Sailor Families: A Preliminary Research Report," Part II, in N. Anderson (ed.), *op. cit.*, II, 115–137.

7. Urie Bronfenbrenner, "The Psychological Costs of Quality and Equality in Education," *Child Development*, XXXVIII, No. 4 (1967), 909–925.

8. Urie Bronfenbrenner, "The Changing American Child," and "Toward a Theoretical Model for the Analysis of Parent-Child Relationships in a Social Context," in John C. Glidewell (ed.), *Parental Attitudes and Child Behavior* (Springfield, Ill.: Charles C Thomas, 1961), 96–109.

9. Bronfenbrenner, "The Changing American Child," 7.

10. Bronfenbrenner, "Toward a Theoretical Model."

11. Cited in *Literaturnaya Gazeta*, January 25, 1967, No. 4, 10.

12. E. Franklin Frazier, *The Negro in the United States*, rev. ed. (New York: The Macmillan Company, 1957); and Bronfenbrenner, "The Psychological Costs of Quality and Equality in Education."

13. Bronfenbrenner, "Soviet Studies of Personality Development and Socialization."

14. Solomon E. Asch, "Studies of Independence and Conformity: A Minority of One Against the Unanimous Majority," *Psychological Monographs*, LXX, No. 9 (1956), Whole No. 416; Morton Deutsch and Harold G. Gerard, "A study of Normative and Informational Social Influence upon Individual Judgment," *Journal of Abnormal and Social Psycology*, LI (1955), 629–636; Stanley Milgram, "Group Pressure and Action Against a Person," *Journal of Abnormal and Social Psychology*, LXIX (1964), 137–143.

15. Ruth W. Berenda, *The Influence of the Group on the Judgements of Children* (New York: King's Crown Press, 1950); M. S. Neimark, "O sootnoshenii osoznavaemikh i neosoznovaemikh motivov v povedenii, kharakterizuyushchem napravlennost lichnosti podrostkov [On the Relationship of Conscious and Unconscious Motives in the Behavior Characterizing the Orientation of the Personality in Adolescence]," *Voprosi Psikhologii* [*Problems of Psychology*], V (1968), 102–110; Muzafer Sherif *et al.*, *Intergroup Conflict and Cooperation: The Robbers Cave Experiment* (Norman: University of Oklahoma Book Exchange, 1961).

16. Deutsch and Gerard, *op. cit.*

17. Asch, *op. cit.*

18. Deutsch and Gerard, *op. cit.*, 631.
19. Urie Bronfenbrenner, "Upbringing in Collective Settings in Switzerland and the U.S.S.R.," *Proceedings of the XVIII International Congress of Psychology, Washington, D.C., August 1963* (Amsterdam: North-Holland Publishing Company, 1964), 159–161.
20. Urie Bronfenbrenner, "Response to Pressure from Peers versus Adults Among Soviet and American School Children," in Urie Bronfenbrenner (chm.), *Social Factors in the Development of Personality*, Symposium 35 presented at the XVIII International Congress of Psychology, Moscow, August, 1966, 7–18; reprinted in *International Journal of Psychology*, II (1967), 199–207. Bronfenbrenner *et al.*, "Adults and Peers as Sources of Conformity and Autonomy," paper presented at the Conference on Socialization for Competence, sponsored by the Social Science Research Council, Puerto Rico, April, 1965. Edward C. Devereux, Jr., "Authority, Guilt, and Conformity to Adult Standards Among German School Children," a Pilot Experimental Study (Unpublished MS., Department of Child Development, Cornell University, 1967). Robert R. Rodgers, Urie Bronfenbrenner, and Edward C. Devereux, Jr., "Standards of Social Behavior Among Children in Four Cultures," *International Journal of Psychology*, III, No. 1 (1968), 31–41.
21. Bronfenbrenner, "Upbringing in Collective Settings in Switzerland and the U.S.S.R."
22. Rodgers, Bronfenbrenner, and Devereux, *op. cit.*
23. S. G. Strumilin, "Rabochy byt i kommunizm [The Worker's Way of Life and Communism]," *Novy Mir*, VII (1960), 203–220.
24. V. N. Kolbanovsky, "Rabochy byt i kommunizm [The Worker's Way of Life and Communism]," *Novy Mir*, II (1961), 276–282.
25. A. G. Kharchev, "Semya i kommunizm [The Family and Communism," *Kommunist*, VII (1960), 53–63; his "O roli semyi v kommunistichesnom vospitanii [On the Role of the Family in Communist Upbringing]," *Sovetskaya pedagogika [Soviet Pedagogy]*, V (1963), 62–72; and *Brak i semia v S.S.S.R. [Marriage and the Family in the U.S.S.R.]* (Moscow: Novosti Press Agency Publishing House, 1964). N. Solovev, *Semya v sovetskom obshchestve [The Family in Soviet Society]* (Moscow: Izdatelstvo Politichesokoi Literatury [The Publishing House of Political Literature], 1962).

A. Levshin, "Malchik-muzhchina-otets (Boy-Man-Father), *Semya i shkola,* II (1964), 2–5.

26. Kharchev, "On the Role of the Family," 63.
27. *Pravda,* April 5, 1961.
28. Solovev, *op. cit.,* 120.
29. See Bronfenbrenner, "The Changing American Child."
30. See Edward C. Devereux, Jr., Urie Bronfenbrenner, and George J. Suci, "Patterns of Parent Behavior in America and West Germany: A Cross-National Comparison," *International Social Science Journal,* XIV, No. 3 (1962), 488–506.
31. See Edward C. Devereux, Jr., Urie Bronfenbrenner, and Robert R. Rodgers, "Child Rearing in England and the United States: A Cross-National Comparison," *Journal of Marriage and the Family,* XXXI, No. 2 (1969), 257–270.
32. L. I. Novikova, "Vospitanie lichnosti v kollektive [The Development of Personality in the Collective]," *Sovetskaya pedagogika [Soviet Pedagogy],* XXXX, No. 3 (1967), 98–117.
33. *Ibid.,* 115, 109.
34. *Ibid.,* 100.
35. F. F. Korolev, *Razvitie osnovnikh idei sovetskoi pedagogiki [The Development of the Basic Ideas of Soviet Pedagogy]* (Moscow: Znanie, 1968).
36. *Pravda,* April 5, 1961, 6.

NOTES TO CHAPTER 4

1. Herbert Wright *et al.,* "Children's Behavior in Communities Differing in Size" (Unpublished MS., Department of Psychology, University of Kansas, 1969).
2. Urie Bronfenbrenner, "Socialization and Social Class Through Time and Space," in Eleanor E. Maccoby, Theodore M. Newcomb, and Eugene L. Hartley (eds.), *Readings in Social Psychology* (New York: Holt, Rinehart & Winston, 1958), 400–425 (London: Methuen).
3. *Ibid.,* 424.
4. Edward C. Devereux, Jr., Urie Bronfenbrenner, and George J. Suci, "Patterns of Parent Behavior in America and West Germany: A Cross-National Comparison," *International Social Science Journal,* XIV, No. 3 (1962), 488–506.
5. *Wall Street Journal* (New York), April 19, 1967.
6. John C. Condry, Jr., Michael L. Siman, and Urie Bronfenbrenner, "Characteristics of Peer- and Adult-Oriented Children" (Unpublished MS., Department of Child Development, Cornell University, 1968).

7. Leo Bogart, "American Television: A Brief Survey of Research Findings," *Journal of Social Issues*, XVIII (1962), 36–42.

8. Lotte Bailyn, "Mass Media and Children: A Study of Exposure Habits and Cognitive Effects," *Psychological Monographs*, Whole No. 471 (1959).

9. Hilde T. Himmelweit, A. N. Oppenheim, and Pamela Vince, *Television and the Child* (New York: Oxford University Press, 1958).

10. Paul A. Witty, P. Kinsella, and A. Coomer, "A Summary of Yearly Studies of Televiewing—1949–1963," *Elementary English*, October, 1963, 590–597.

11. Robert O. Blood, Jr., "Social Class and Family Control of Television Viewing," *Merrill-Palmer Quarterly of Behavior and Development*, III (1961), 205–222; Bailyn, *op. cit.*

12. *The Republic*, translated by Francis M. Cornford (New York: Oxford University Press, 1958), Book II, 69.

13. Urie Bronfenbrenner, "The Changing American Child," *Journal of Social Issues*, XVII, No. 1 (1961), 6–18.

14. George R. Bach, "Father-Fantasies and Father-Typing in Father-Separated Children," *Child Development*, XVII (1946), 63–79; Pauline S. Sears, "Doll Play Aggression in Normal Young Children: Influence of Sex, Age, Sibling Status, Father's Absence," *Psychological Monographs*, LXV, No. 6 (1951), Whole No. 323; Robert R. Sears, Margaret H. Pintler, and Pauline S. Sears, "Effects of Father Separation on Preschool Children's Doll Play Aggression," *Child Development*, XVII (1946), 219-243; Lois M. Stolz, *Father Relations of War-born Children* (Palo Alto, Cal.: Stanford University Press, 1954).

15. Erik Gronseth, "The Impact of Father Absence in Sailor Families upon the Personality Structure and Social Adjustment of Adult Sailor Sons," Part I, in N. Anderson (ed.), *Studies of the Family*, 2 vols. (Göttingen: Vandenhoeck and Ruprecht, 1957), II, 97–114; David B. Lynn and William L. Sawrey, "The Effects of Father-Absence on Norwegian Boys and Girls," *Journal of Abnormal and Social Psychology*, LIX (1959), 258–262; Per O. Tiller, "Father Absence and Personality Development of Children in Sailor Families: A Preliminary Research Report," Part II, in N. Anderson (ed.), *op. cit.*, II, 115–137, and "Father Separation and Adolescence" (Oslo: Institute for Social Research, 1961, mimeographed).

16 Walter Mischel, "Father-Absence and Delay of Gratification: Cross-cultural Comparison," *Journal of Abnormal and So-*

cial Psychology, LXIII (1961), 116–124.

17. A. Barclay and D. R. Cusumano, "Father Absence, Cross-Sex Identity, and Field Dependent Behavior in Male Adolescents," *Child Development*, XXXVIII (1967), 243–250; Roger V. Burton and John W. M. Whiting, "The Absent Father and Cross-Sex Identity," *Merrill-Palmer Quarterly*, VII (1961), 85–95; C. Kuckenberg, "Effect of Early Father Absence on Scholastic Aptitude" (Unpublished doctoral dissertation, Harvard University, 1963).

18. Bernard C. Rosen, "Conflicting Group Membership: A Study of Parent-Peer Group Cross Pressures," *American Sociological Review*, XX (1955), 151–161; Mason Haire and F. Morrison, "School Children's Perceptions of Labor and Management," *Journal of Social Psychology*, XLVI (1957), 179–197.

19. Charles E. Bowerman and John W. Kinch, "Changes in Family and Peer Orientation of Children Between the 4th and 10th Grades," *Social Forces*, XXXVII, No. 3 (1959), 206–211.

20. John C. Condry, Jr., and Michael L. Siman, "An Experimental Study of Adult versus Peer Orientation" (Unpublished MS, Department of Child Development, Cornell University, 1968).

21. James S. Coleman, *The Adolescent Society* (London: Collier-Macmillan, 1961).

22. *Ibid.*, 265.

23. James S. Coleman *et al.*, *Equality of Educational Opportunity* (Washington, D.C.: U.S. Government Printing Office, 1966).

24. *Ibid.*, 304.

25. United States Commission on Civil Rights, *Racial Isolation in the Public Schools* (Washington, D.C.: U.S. Government Printing Office, 1967).

26. *Ibid.*, 100.

27. Thomas F. Pettigrew, "Race and Equal Educational Opportunity," paper presented at the Symposium on the Implications of the Coleman Report on *Equality of Educational Opportunity* at the annual convention of the American Psychological Association, 1967.

28. Albert Bandura and Aletha C. Huston, "Identification as a Process of Incidental Learning," *Journal of Abnormal and Social Psychology*, LXIII (1961), 311–318; Albert Bandura, Dorothea Ross, and Sheila A. Ross, "Transmission of Aggression Through Imitation of Aggressive Models," *Journal*

of *Abnormal and Social Psychology*, LXII (1961), 575–582; Albert Bandura and Richard H. Walters, *Social Learning and Personality Development* (London: Holt, Rinehart & Winston, 1963).

29. Albert Bandura, Dorothea Ross, and Sheila A. Ross, "Imitation of Film-mediated Aggressive Models," *Journal of Abnormal and Social Psychology*, LXVI (1963), 3–11.

30. Television Information Office Release SM 15, 1963.

31. David J. Hicks, "Imitation and Retention of Film-mediated Aggressive Peer and Adult Models," *Journal of Personality and Social Psychology*, II (1965), 97–100.

32. Leonard D. Eron, "Relationship of TV Viewing Habits and Aggressive Behavior in Children," *Journal of Abnormal and Social Psychology*, LXVII (1963), 193–196.

33. Richard H. Walters and E. Llewellyn Thomas, "Enhancement of Punitiveness by Visual and Audiovisual Displays," *Canadian Journal of Psychology*, XVII, No. 2 (1963), 244–255; Richard H. Walters, E. Llewellyn Thomas, and Charles W. Acker, "Enhancement of Punitive Behavior by Audiovisual Displays," *Science*, CXXXVI (1962), 872–873.

34. Leonard Berkowitz and Edna Rawlings, "Effects of Film Violence on Inhibitions against Subsequent Aggression," *Journal of Abnormal and Social Psychology*, LXVI (1963), 405–412; Leonard Berkowitz, R. Corwin, and M. Heironimus, "Film Violence and Subsequent Aggressive Tendencies," *Public Opinion Quarterly*, XXVII (1963), 217–229; Leonard Berkowitz (ed.), *Advances in Experimental Social Psychology*, 2 vols. (London: Academic Press, 1965); Leonard Berkowitz and R. G. Geen, "Film Violence and the Cue Properties of Available Targets," *Journal of Personality and Social Psychology*, III (1966), 525–530; R. G. Geen and Leonard Berkowitz, "Name-mediated Aggressive Cue Properties," *Journal of Personality*, XXXIV (1966), 456–465.

35. Leonard Berkowitz and J. A. Green, "The Stimulus Qualities of the Scapegoat," *Journal of Abnormal and Social Psychology*, LXIV (1962), 293–301.

36. D. P. Hartman, "The Influence of Symbolically Modeled Instrumental Aggression and Pain Cues on the Disinhibition of Aggressive Behavior" (Unpublished doctoral dissertation, Stanford University, 1965); summarized in Leonard Berkowitz (ed.), *Advances in Experimental Social Psychology*, *op. cit.*, II, 22–24.

37. Albert Bandura, "Vicarious Processes: A Case of No-Trial Learn-

ing," in Leonard Berkowitz (ed.), *Advances in Experimental Social Psychology, op. cit.,* II, 1–55; quotation on page 23.

38. Cf. Seymour Feshbach, "The Function of Aggression and the Regulation of Aggressive Drive," *Psychological Review,* LXXI (1964), 257–272; Berkowitz, *Advances in Experimental Social Psychology,* and *Aggression: A Social Psychological Analysis* (Maidenhead: McGraw-Hill, 1962).

39. Hartman, *op. cit.,* 24.

40. Geen and Berkowitz, *op. cit.*

41. Berkowitz, *Advances in Experimental Social Psychology,* 318.

42. Stanley Milgram, "Group Pressure and Action against a Person," *Journal of Abnormal and Social Psychology,* LXIX (1964), 137–143.

43. Urie Bronfenbrenner *et al.,* "Adults and Peers as Sources of Conformity and Autonomy," paper presented at the Conference on Socialization for Competence, sponsored by the Social Science Research Council, Puerto Rico, April, 1965.

44. Edward C. Devereux, Jr., Urie Bronfenbrenner, and Robert R. Rodgers, "Child Rearing in England and the United States, a Cross-National Comparison," *Journal of Marriage and the Family,* XXXI, No. 2 (1969).

45. Lee Charlotte Lee, "The Development of Moral Judgment and Cognition from Childhood through Adolescence: A Test of Piagetian Theory" (Doctoral dissertation, Ohio State University, 1968).

46. A. S. Makarenko, *The Road to Life* (Moscow: Foreign Languages Publishing House, 1955).

47. L. I. Novikova, "Vospitanie lichnosti v kollektive [The Development of Personality in the Collective]," *Sovetskaya Pedagogika [Soviet Pedagogy],* XXXI, No. 3 (1967), 98–117; the quotation is from page 103.

48. William Golding, *Lord of the Flies* (London: Faber 1954; Penguin).

Notes to Chapter 5

1. CBS-TV Reports, "Hunger in the U.S.A.," Summer, 1968.

2. A. Frederick North, "Pediatric Care in Project Head Start," in Jerome Hellmuth (ed.), *The Disadvantaged Child:* Volume II, *Head Start and Early Intervention* (Seattle: Special Child Publications, 1968).

3. *Advancement of Knowledge for the Nation's Health,* a report
   prepared for the President of the United States by the staffs
   of the National Institutes of Health (Bethesda, Md.: National Institutes of Health, 1967), 149–150.
4. *Infant Mortality: A Challenge to the Nation* (Washington,
   D.C.: U.S. Department of Health, Education and Welfare,
   Children's Bureau, 1966), 1.
5. *Advancement of Knowledge for the Nation's Health,* 150.
6. Hilda Knobloch *et al.,* "Neural Psychiatric Sequelae of Prematurity," *Journal of the American Medical Association,*
   CLXI (1956), 581–585; Benjamin Pasamanick and Hilda
   Knobloch, "The Contribution of Some Organic Factors to
   School Retardation in Negro Children," *Journal of Negro
   Education,* XXVII (1958), 4–9; Benjamin Pasamanick,
   Hilda Knobloch, and A. M. Lilienfeld, "Socioeconomic
   Status and Some Precursors of Neuropsychiatric Disorder,"
   American Journal of Orthopsychiatrics, XXVI (1956),
   594–601.
7. A. A. Kawi and Benjamin Pasamanick, "Prenatal and Parental
   Factors in the Development of Childhood Reading Disor-
   ders," *Monographs of the Society for Research in Child
   Development,* XXIV, No. 4 (1959), Serial No. 73.
8. *Ibid.,* 19.
9. Pasamanick and Knobloch, *op. cit.,* 7.
10. Albert Bandura and Frederick J. McDonald, "The Influence of
    Social Reinforcement and the Behavior of Models in Shap-
    ing Children's Moral Judgments," *Journal of Abnormal
    and Social Psychology,* II (1965), 698–705.
11. Richard H. Walters, Norma V. Bowen, and Ross D. Parke, "Ex-
    perimentally Induced Disinhibition of Sexual Responses"
    (Unpublished MS, Department of Psychology, University
    of Waterloo, Canada, 1963); Albert Bandura and Richard
    H. Walters, *Social Learning and Personality Development*
    (London: Holt, Rinehart & Winston, 1963).
12. A. Freed *et al.,* "Stimulus and Background Factors in Sign Vio-
    lation," *Journal of Personality,* XXIII (1955), 499; Donald
    Kimbrell and Robert R. Blake, "Motivational Factors in the
    Violation of a Prohibition," *Journal of Abnormal and Social
    Psychology,* LVI (1958), 132–133; Monroe Lefkowitz,
    Robert R. Blake, and Jane S. Mouton, "Status Factors in
    Pedestrian Violation of Traffic Signals," *Journal of Ab-
    normal and Social Psychology,* LI (1955), 704–705.
13. Albert Bandura, Dorothea Ross, and Sheila A. Ross, "Transmis-

sion of Aggression Through Imitation of Aggressive Models," *Journal of Abnormal and Social Psychology*, LXIII (1961), 575–582, and their "Imitation of Film-mediated Aggressive Models," *Journal of Abnormal and Social Psychology*, LXVI (1963), 3–11.

14. Albert Bandura, Dorothea Ross, and Sheila A. Ross, "Vicarious Reinforcement and Imitative Learning," *Journal of Abnormal and Social Psychology*, LXVII (1963), 601–607; Albert Bandura, "Influence of Models' Reinforcement Contingencies on the Acquisition of Imitative Responses," *Journal of Personality and Social Psychology*, I (1965), 589–595, and "Vicarious Processes: A Case of No-Trial Learning," in Leonard Berkowitz (ed.), *Advances in Experimental Social Psychology*, 2 vols. (New York and London: Academic Press, 1965), II, 1–55.

15. Mary A. Rosekrans, "Imitation in Children as a Function of Perceived Similarities to a Social Model of Vicarious Reinforcement," *Journal of Personality and Social Psychology*, VII (1967), 307–315; Willard W. Hartup, "Peer Interaction and Social Organization," in Paul H. Mussen (ed.), *Manual of Child Psychology* (New York: John Wiley & Sons, 1969); A. A. Benton, "Effects of the Timing of Negative Response Consequences on the Observational Learning of Resistance to Temptation in Children," *Dissertation Abstracts*, XXVII, No. 6B (1966), 2153–2154.

16. D. Grosser, Norman Polansky, and Ronald Lippitt, "A Laboratory Study of Behavioral Contagion," *Human Relations*, IV (1951), 115–142.

17. Walter Mischel and Robert M. Liebert, "Effects of Discrepancies Between Observed and Imposed Reward Criteria on Their Acquisition and Transmission," *Journal of Personality and Social Psychology*, III (1966), 45–53; Albert Bandura, Joan E. Grusec, Frances L. Menlove, "Vicarious Extinction of Avoidance Behavior," *Journal of Personality and Social Psychology*, V (1967), 16–23.

18. Albert Bandura and Walter Mischel, "Modification of Self-Imposed Delay of Reward Through Exposure to Live and Symbolic Models," *Journal of Personality and Social Psychology*, II (1965), 698–705.

19. Walter Mischel, "Preference for Delayed Reinforcement and Social Responsibility," *Journal of Abnormal and Social Psychology*, LXII (1961), 1–7, and "Delay of Gratification, Need for Achievement, and Acquiescence in Another Culture," *ibid.*, 543–552, and, "Father Absence and Delay of

Gratification: Cross-Cultural Comparisons," *Journal of Abnormal and Social Psychology*, LXIII (1961), 116–124.

20. Aletha H. Stein, "Imitation of Resistance to Temptation," *Child Development*, XXXVIII, No. 1 (1967), 157–169.

21. Kimbrell and Blake, *op. cit.*

22. James H. Bryan and Mary A. Test, "Models and Helping: Naturalistic Studies in Aiding Behavior," *Journal of Personality and Social Psychology*, VI (1967), 400–407.

23. M. A. Test and James H. Bryan, "Dependency, Models, and Reciprocity" (Unpublished MS, Department of Psychology, Northwestern University, 1966).

24. David L. Rosenhan and G. M. White, "Observation and Rehearsal as Determinants of Prosocial Behavior," *Journal of Personality and Social Psychology*, V (1967), 424–431.

25. Bandura, Dorothea Ross, and Sheila A. Ross, "Imitation of Film-mediated Aggressive Models," 3–11.

26. Neal E. Miller and John Dollard, *Social Learning and Imitation* (New Haven and London: Yale University Press, 1941).

27. Donald M. Baer and J. A. Sherman, "Reinforcement Control of Generalized Imitation in Young Children," *Journal of Experimental Child Psychology*, I (1964), 37–49; Donald M. Baer, R. F. Peterson, and J. A. Sherman, "The Development of Imitation by Reinforcing Behavioral Similarity to a Model," *Journal of the Experimental Analysis of Behavior*, X (1967), 405–416.

28. Albert Bandura, *Principles of Behavioral Modification* (New York: Holt, Rinehart & Winston, 1968).

29. Reuben M. Baron, "Social Reinforcement Effects as a Function of Social Reinforcement History," *Psychological Review*, LXXIII (1966), 527–540.

30. M. S. Gerst, "Symbolic Coding Operations in Observational Learning" (Unpublished doctoral dissertation, Stanford University, 1968); Urie Bronfenbrenner, "Early Deprivation: A Cross-Species Analysis," in Grant Newton and Seymour Levine (eds.), *Early Experience and Behavior* (Springfield, Ill.: Charles C Thomas, 1968), 627–764; Albert Bandura, Joan E. Grusec, and Frances L. Menlove, "Observational Learning as a Function of Symbolization and Incentive Set," *Child Development*, XXXVII (1966), 499–506.

31. Lefkowitz, Blake, and Mouton, *op. cit.*; Bernard Mausner, "Studies in Social Interaction: III, Effect of Variation in One Partner's Prestige on the Interaction of Observer Pairs," *Journal of Applied Psychology*, XXXVII (1953),

391–393; Milton E. Rosenbaum and Irving F Tucker, "The Competence of the Model and the Learning of Imitation and Nonimitation," *Journal of Experimental Psychology*, LXIII, No. 2 (1962), 183–190.

32. Albert Bandura, Dorothea Ross, and Sheila A. Ross, "A Comparative Test of the Status Envy, Social Power, and Secondary Reinforcement Theories of Identificatory Learning," *Journal of Abnormal and Social Psychology*, LXVII (1963), 527–534.

33. Albert Bandura and Aletha C. Huston, "Identification as a Process of Incidental Learning," *Journal of Abnormal and Social Psychology*, LXIII (1961), 311–318; J. E. Grusec, "Model Characteristics, Techniques of Punishment, and Reinforcement Contingency as Antecedents of Self-Criticism" (Unpublished doctoral dissertation, Stanford University, 1965); J. E. Grusec and Walter Mischel, "The Model's Characteristics as Determinants of Social Learning" (Unpublished MS, Department of Psychology, Stanford University, 1965); Paul H. Mussen and Ann L. Parker, "Mother-Nurturance and Girl's Incidental Imitative Learning," *Journal of Personality and Social Psychology*, II (1965), 94–97.

34. E.g., Urie Bronfenbrenner, "The Changing American Child," *Journal of Social Issues*, XVII, No. 1 (1961), 6–18; Robert R. Sears, Lucy Rau, and Richard Alpert, *Identification in Child Rearing* (Stanford, Cal.: Stanford University Press, 1965); John A. Clausen, "Family Structure, Socialization, and Personality," in Lois Wladis Hoffman and Martin L. Hoffman, *Review of Child Development Research*, 2 vols. (New York: Russell Sage Foundation; I, 1964; II, 1966), II, 1–54; Albert Bandura and Richard H. Walters, *Adolescent Aggression* (New York: Ronald Press, 1959), and their *Social Learning and Personality Development;* Willard W. Hartup, *op. cit.*

35. Rosekrans, *op. cit.*

36. Eugene Burnstein, Ezra Stotland, and Alvin F. Zander, "Similarity to a Model and Self-Evaluation," *Journal of Abnormal and Social Psychology*, LII (1961), 257–264.

37. Ezra Stotland, Alvin F. Zander, and Thomas Natsoulas, "Generalization of Interpersonal Similarity," *Journal of Abnormal and Social Psychology*, LXI (1962), 250–256; Ezra Stotland and Robert E. Dunn, "Identification, 'Oppositeness,' Authoritarianism, Self-Esteem, and Birth Order," *Psychological Monographs*, LXXVI, No. 9 (1962),

Whole No. 528, and, "Empathy, Self-Esteem and Birth Order," *Journal of Abnormal and Social Psychology*, LXVI (1962, 532–540; Ezra Stotland and Max L. Hillmer, Jr., "Identification, Authoritarian Defensiveness and Self-Esteem," *Journal of Abnormal and Social Psychology*, LXIV (1962), 334–342.

38. Albert Bandura, "Externalization of the Superego: Comments on Conduct and Conscience," in Martin Hoffman (ed.), *Character Development in the Child* (Chicago: Aldine, in press), and his "Behavioral Psychotherapy," *Scientific American*, CCXVI, No. 3 (1967), 78–86.

39. Bandura, "Influence of Model's Reinforcement Contingencies," and "Vicarious Processes"; Bandura, D. Ross, and S. A. Ross, "Vicarious Reinforcement and Imitative Learning."

40. Bandura, "Influence of Model's Reinforcement Contingencies."

41. Harriet L. Rheingold, Jacob L. Gewirtz, and Helen W. Ross, "Social Conditioning of Vocalizations in the Infant," *Journal of Comparative and Physiological Psychology*, LII (1959), 68–73.

42. Albert I. Prince, "Relative Prestige and the Verbal Conditioning of Children," *American Psychologist*, XVII (1962), 594–601.

43. Urie Bronfenbrenner, "The Psychological Costs of Quality and Equality in Education," *Child Development*, XXXVIII, No. 4 (1967), 909–925.

44. Julian B. Rotter, "Generalized Expectancies for Internal versus External Control of Reinforcement," *Psychological Monographs*, I (1966), Whole No. 609; Herbert M. Lefcourt and Gordon W. Ladwig, "The American Negro: A Profile in Expectancies," *Journal of Personality and Social Psychology*, I (1965), 377–380; Herbert M. Lefcourt, "Internal versus External Control of Reinforcement: A Review," *Psychological Bulletins*, LXV (1966), 206–220.

45. Esther Battle, "Motivational Determinants of Academic Task Persistence," *Journal of Abnormal and Social Psychology*, II (1965), 209–218; June E. Chance, "Internal Control of Reinforcements and the School Learning Process," paper given at Society for Research in Child Development meeting, Minneapolis, 1965; Vaughn J. Crandall, Walter Katkowsky, and Anne L. Preston, "Motivational and Ability Determinants of Young Children's Intellectual Achievement Behaviors," *Child Development*, XXXIII (1962), 643–661; Virginia C. Crandall, Walter Katkovsky, and

Vaughn J. Crandall, "Children's Beliefs in Their Own Control of Reinforcements in Intellectual-Academic Achievement Situations," *Child Development*, XXXVI (1965), 91–109; Russell Eisenman and J. J. Blatt, "Birth Order and Sex Differences in Academic Achievement and Internal-External Control," *Journal of General Psychology*, LXXVIII (1968), 279–285; P. E. McGhee and Virginia C. Crandall, "Beliefs in Internal-External Control of Reinforcements and Academic Performance, *Child Development*, XXXIX (1968), 91–102.

46. James S. Coleman *et al.*, *Equality of Educational Opportunity* (Washington, D.C.: U.S. Government Printing Office, 1966), 321.

47. Robert Rosenthal, "The Effect of the Experimenter on the Results of Psychological Research," in B. A. Maher (ed.), *Progress in Experimental Personality Research*, 4 vols. (New York: Academic Press, 1964), I, 79–114, and *Experimenter Effects in Behavioral Research* (New York: Appleton, 1966); Robert Rosenthal and Lenore Jacobson, *Pygmalion in the Classroom* (New York: Holt, Rinehart & Winston, 1968).

48. Rosenthal and Jacobson, *Pygmalion in the Classroom*, 20.

49. Sears, Rau, and Alpert, *op. cit.*; Bandura and Walters, *Adolescent Aggression* and *Social Learning and Personality Development*; Clausen, *op. cit.*; Loretta K. Cass, "An Investigation of Parent-Child Relationships in Terms of Awareness, Identification, Projection, and Control," *American Journal of Orthopsychiatry*, XXII (1952), 305–313; Virginia C. Crandall, "The Reinforcements Effects of Adult Reactions and Nonreactions on Children's Achievement Expectations," *Child Development*, XXXIV (1963), 335–354; Walter Emmerich, "Parental Identification in Young Children," *Genetic Psychology Monographs*, LX (1959), 257–308; Susan W. Gray and Rupert Klaus, "The Assessment of Parental Identification, *Genetic Psychology Monographs*, LIV (1956), 87–114; E. Mavis Hetherington, "A Developmental Study of the Effects of Sex of the Dominant Parent on Sex-Role Performance, Identification, and Imitation in Children," *Journal of Personality and Social Psychology*, II (1965), 188–194; Mussen and Parker, *op. cit.*

50. Bronfenbrenner, "Early Deprivation: A Cross-Species Analysis."

51. Harold M. Skeels, "Adult Status of Children with Contrasting Early Life Experiences," *Monographs of the Society for Research in Child Development*, XXXI (1966), Serial No. 105.
52. Bronfenbrenner, "Early Deprivation: A Cross-Species Analysis."
53. Muzafer Sherif, "Superordinate Goals in the Reduction of Intergroup Tensions," *American Journal of Sociology*, LIII (1958), 349–356.
54. Muzafer Sherif, "Experiments in Group Conflict," *Scientific American*, CXCV, No. 2 (1956), 54–58; Muzafer Sherif et al., *Intergroup Conflict and Cooperation: The Robbers Cave Experiment* (Norman: University of Oklahoma Book Exchange, 1961).
55. Sherif et al., *op. cit.*
56. Elton B. McNeil, "Waging Experimental War: A Review," *Journal of Conflict Resolution*, VI, No. 1 (1962), 77–81; quotation from page 77.
57. Sherif, "Experiments in Group Conflict," 54–58.
58. Urie Bronfenbrenner, "Soviet Studies of Personality Development and Socialization," in Raymond Bauer (ed.), *Some Views of Soviet Psychology* (Washington, D.C.: American Psychological Association, 1962), 63–86.
59. M. S. Neimark, "O sootnoshenii osoznavaemikh i neosoznavaemikh motivov v povedenii, kharakterizuyushchem napravlennost lichnosti podrostkov [On the Relationship of Conscious and Unconscious Motives in Behavior Characterizing the Orientation of the Personality in Adolescence]," *Voprosi psikhologii* [*Problems of Psychology*], V (1968), 102–110.

Notes to Chapter 6

1. N. L. Gage, *Handbook of Research and Teaching* (Chicago: Rand McNally, 1963).
2. Martin Deutsch, "Minority Group and Class Status as Related to Social and Personality Factors in Scholastic Achievement," *Monograph of the Society for Applied Anthropology*, II (1960), 1–32.

Index

Advancement of Knowledge for the Nation's Health, 122, 179 n.3
Acker, Charles W., 110, 177 n.33
Alpert, Richard, 133, 139, 182 n.34, 184 n.49
Asch, Solomon E., 75, 172 n.14
Auslender, L. B., 62, 170 n.21

Bach, George R., 71, 104, 171 n.5, 175 n.14
Baer, Donald M., 131, 181 n.27
Bailyn, Lotte, 102, 175 n.8
Bandura, Albert, 109, 110, 113, 114, 125, 126, 131, 132, 134, 139, 176 n.28, 177 n.29, 37, 179 n.10, 11, 13, 180 n.14, 17, 18, 181 n.25, 28, 30, 182 n.32, 33, 34, 183 n.38, 39, 40
Barclay, A., 104, 176 n.17
Baron, Reuben M., 131, 181 n.29
Battle, Esther, 137, 183 n.45
Becker, Wesley C., 70, 171 n.2
Benton, A. A., 126, 180 n.15
Berenda, Ruth W., 75, 172 n.15
Berkowitz, Leonard, 112, 113, 114, 177 n.34, 35, 178 n.38
Blake, Robert R., 126, 127, 132, 179 n.12
Blatt, J. J., 137, 184 n.45
Blood, Robert O., Jr., 102, 175 n.11
Bogart, Leo, 102, 175 n.7

Boldyrev, N.I., 26–36, 51, 170 n.4, 10
Bowen, Norma V., 126, 179 n. 11
Bowerman, Charles E., 105, 176 n.19
Bronfenbrenner, U., 15, 70, 71, 72, 74, 77, 85, 98, 101, 104, 116, 133, 137, 139, 140, 151, 171 n.2, 4, 172 n.7–10, 12, 13, 173 n.19–22, 174 n.30–31, n.2, 4, 6, 175 n.13, 178 n.43, 44, 181 n.30, 182 n.34, 183 n.43, 184 n.50, 185 n.52, 58
Bryan, James H., 127, 128, 181 n.22, 23
Burnstein, Eugene, 134, 182 n.36
Burton, Roger V., 104, 176 n.17

Caldwell, Bettye M., 70, 171 n.2
Cass, Loretta K., 139, 184 n.49
CBS-TV Reports, 121, 178 n.1
Chance, June E., 137, 183 n.45
Clausen, John A., 70, 133, 139, 171 n.2, 182 n.34
Coleman, James S., 105, 106, 107, 137, 138, 176 n.21, 23, 27, 184 n.46
Commentary on Bandura's *Look* Article, 110, 177 n.29
Condry, John C., Jr., 101, 105, 174 n.6, 176 n.20
Coomer, A., 102, 175 n.10
Corwin, R., 111, 177 n.34

Crandall, Vaughn J., 137, 183 n.45

Crandall, Virginia C., 137, 139, 183 n.45, 184 n.49

Cusumano, D. R., 104, 176 n.17

Deutsch, Martin, 153, 185 n.2

Deutsch, Morton, 75, 76, 172 n.14

Devereux, Edward C., Jr., 77, 80, 81, 85, 98, 116, 173 n.20, 22, 174 n.30–31, 174 n.4, 178 n.44

Dollard, John, 131, 181 n.26

Dunn, Robert E., 134, 182 n.37

Eisenman, Russell, 137, 184 n.45

Emmerich, Walter, 139, 184 n.49

Eron, Leonard D., 110, 177 n.32

Feshbach, Seymour, 113, 178 n.38

Frazier, E. Franklin, 73, 172 n.12

Freed, A., 126, 179 n.12

Gage, N. L., 153, 185 n.1

Geen, R. G., 111, 114, 177 n.34

Gerard, Harold G., 75, 76, 172 n.14

Gerst, M. S., 131, 181 n.30

Gewirtz, Jacob S., 135, 183 n.41

Golding, William, 118, 178 n.48

Gray, Susan W., 139, 184 n.49

Green, J. A., 111, 112, 177 n.35

Gronseth, Erik, 71, 104, 171 n.6, 175 n.15

Grosser, D., 126, 127, 180 n.16

Grusec, Joan E., 127, 131, 132, 180 n.16, 181 n.30, 182 n.33

Haire, Mason, 105, 176 n.18

Hartman, D. P., 112, 177 n.36

Hartup, Willard W., 70, 126, 133, 171 n.2, 180 n.15

Heironimus, M., 111, 177 n.34

Hetherington, E. Mavis, 139, 184 n.49

Hicks, David J., 110, 177 n.31

Hillmer, Max L., Jr., 134, 183 n.37

Himmelweit, Hilde T., 102, 175 n.9

Huston, Aletha C., 109, 132, 176 n.28, 182 n.33

Jacobson, Lenore, 139, 184 n.47

Kairov, I. A., 4, 37, 169 n.2

Kassof, A., 36, 170 n.7

Katkowsky, Walter, 137, 183 n.45

Kawi, A. A., 123, 179 n.7

Kharchev, A. G., 83, 84, 173 n.25, 174 n.26

Khodakovsky, L. S., 51, 170 n.10

Kimbrell, Donald, 126, 127, 179 n.12

Kinch, John W., 105, 176 n.19

Kinsella, P., 102, 175 n.10

Klaus, Rupert, 139, 184 n.49

Knobloch, Hilda, 123, 124, 179 n.6

Kolbanovsky, V. N., 83, 173 n.24

Konnikova, T. E., 51, 170 n.10

Korolev, F. F., 88, 174 n.35

Kuckenberg, C., 104, 176 n.17

Ladwig, Gordon W., 137, 183 n.44

Lee, Lee Charlotte, 117, 178 n.45

Lefcourt, Herbert M., 137, 183 n.44

Lefkowitz, Monroe, 126, 132, 179 n.12

Levshin, A., 83, 84, 174 n.25

Levy, David M., 70, 170 n.1

Liebert, Robert M., 127, 180 n.17

Lilienfeld, A. M., 123, 179 n.6

Lippitt, Ronald, 126, 127, 180 n.16

Lynn, David B., 71, 104, 171 n.6, 175 n.15

MacDonald, Frederick J., 125, 179 n.10

Makarenko, A. S., 3, 38, 118, 169 n.1, 170 n.8, 178 n.46

Mausner, Bernard, 132, 181 n.31

McGhee, P. E., 137, 184 n.45

McNeil, Elton B., 145, 185 n.56
Menlove, Frances L., 127, 131, 180 n.17, 181 n.30
Milgram, Stanley, 75, 114, 115, 172 n.14, 178 n.42
Miller, Neal E., 131, 181 n.26
Mischel, Walter, 104, 127, 132, 176 n.16, 180 n.17, 18, 182 n.33
Morrison, F., 105, 176 n.18
Mouton, Jane S., 126, 132, 179 n.12
Mussen, Paul H., 132, 139, 180 n.15, 182 n.33

Natsoulas, Thomas, 134, 182 n.37
Neimark, M. S., 75, 151, 172 n.15, 185 n.59
North, A. Frederick, 121, 122, 178 n.2
Novikova, L. I., 51, 53, 55, 57, 58, 59, 60, 61, 62, 63, 64, 65, 66, 67, 68, 86, 87, 88, 118, 151, 170 n.9, 174 n.32, 178 n.47

Oppenheim, A. N., 102, 175 n.9

Parke, Ross D., 126, 179 n.11
Parker, Ann L., 132, 139, 182 n.33
Pasamanick, Benjamin, 123, 179 n.6, 7
Pechernikova, I. A., 10, 11, 12, 13, 14, 73, 169 n.5
Peterson, R. F., 131, 181 n.27
Pettigrew, Thomas F., 108, 176 n.27
Pintler, Margaret H., 71, 104, 171 n.5, 175 n.14
Plato, 103, 175 n.12
Polansky, Norman, 126, 127, 180 n.16
Preston, Anne, 137, 183 n.45
Prince, Albert I., 135, 136, 183 n.42

Rau, Lucy, 133, 139, 182 n.34
Rawlings, Edna, 111, 177 n.34

Rheingold, Harriet L., 135, 183 n.41
Rodgers, Robert R., 77, 80, 81, 85, 116, 173 n.20, 22, 174 n.31, 178 n.44
Rosekrans, Mary A., 126, 133, 180 n.15
Rosen, Bernard C., 105, 176 n.18
Rosenbaum, Milton E., 132, 182 n.31
Rosenhan, David L., 128, 181 n.24
Rosenthal, Robert, 138, 139, 153, 184 n.47
Ross, Dorothea, 109, 110, 126, 132, 134, 176 n.28, 177 n.29, 179 n.13, 180 n.14, 181 n.25, 182 n.32
Ross, Helen W., 135, 183 n.41
Ross, Sheila A., 109, 110, 126, 132, 134, 135, 176 n.28, 177 n.29, 179 n.13, 180 n.14, 181 n.25, 182 n.32
Rotter, Julian B., 137, 183 n.44

Sawrey, William L., 71, 104, 171 n.6, 175 n.15
Sears, Pauline S., 71, 104, 171 n.5, 175 n.14
Sears, Robert R., 71, 104, 133, 139, 171 n.5, 175 n.14, 182 n.34
Sherif, Muzafer, 75, 144, 145, 147, 172 n.15, 185 n.53, 54
Sherman, J. A., 131, 181 n.27
Siman, M. L., 101, 105, 174 n.6, 176 n.20
Skeels, Harold M., 140, 185 n.51
Solovev, N., 84, 173 n.25
Stein, Aletha H., 127, 181 n.20
Stolz, Lois M., 71, 104, 171 n.5, 175 n.14
Stotland, Ezra, 134, 182 n.36, 37
Strumilin, S. G., 82, 83, 173 n.23
Suci, George J., 77, 85, 98, 116, 174 n.30, 174 n.4
Sukhomlinsky, V. A., 26, 169 n.1
Symonds, Percival M., 70, 170 n.1

Test, M. A., 128, 181 *n*.22, 23
Thomas, E. Llewellyn, 110, 177
   n.33
Tiller, Per O., 71, 104, 171 *n*.6,
   175 *n.15*
Tucker, Irving F., 132, 182 *n.31*

U.S. Children's Bureau, 122, 179
   n.4
U.S. Commission on Civil Rights,
   108, 176 *n.25*

Vince, Pamela, 102, 175 *n.9*
Volkova, E. I., 9, 10, 169 *n.1*

Walters, Richard H., 109, 110,
   126, 133, 139, 176 *n.28*, 177
   n.33, 179 *n.11*, 182 *n.34*
White, G. M., 128, 181 *n* 24
Whiting, John W. M., 104, 176
   n.17
Witty, Paul A., 102, 175 *n.10*
Wright, Herbert, 96, 174 *n.1*

Zaluzhskaya, M. V., 18, 19, 20,
   21, 169 *n.1*
Zander, Alvin, 134, 182 *n.36, 37*

Childhood in Society is an occasional series examining childhood, socialization and education from an interdisciplinary standpoint. The other two volumes already published are *Centuries of Childhood* by Philippe Ariès and *The Discovery of Death in Childhood and After* by Sylvia Anthony.

Centuries of Childhood

Philippe Ariès

The questions around which this book revolves are no less than the origins of modern ideas about the family and about childhood. Before the seventeenth century a child was regarded as a small and inadequate adult; the concept of 'the childish' as something distinct from adults is a creation of the modern world. The change involved far-reaching implications for the family, for education, and for children themselves. 'It will come as no surprise to the reader,' writes Philippe Ariès, 'if these questions take us to the very heart of the great problems of civilization, for we are standing on those frontiers of biology and sociology from which mankind derives its hidden strength.'

Centuries of Childhood is by now a classic. It must surely rank as one of those books which, among changing fashions, emphases and perspectives, retain their power to illuminate our perception of childhood – its possible nature and its relation to other social forms. It is also a subtle and skilful piece of demographic history. In the course of his analysis, Ariès includes much fascinating material on such diverse topics as dress, the history of games and pastimes, attitudes towards sex and early ideas about education.

The Discovery of Death in Childhood and After

Sylvia Anthony

Ben (aged seven), in his mother's bed for a minute or two before breakfast, talking about measles, said happily: 'I'd like to die.' Mother: 'Why?' Ben: 'Because I'd like to be in the same grave as you.'

Among the 'facts of life' encountered by children, the phenomenon of death is probably the most formidable. In this remarkable book Sylvia Anthony both delineates the ways in which children discover and assimilate the concept of death, and establishes the critical importance of that discovery for their subsequent intellectual and emotional maturity. Her study makes vivid and extensive use of children's conversation about death, tracing the developmental pattern from the pre-school child's confusion of death with lack of movement to the adolescent's rational biological conceptualization. By means of this absorbing material the author examines the resemblances of the children's reactions to those of members of other cultures remote from their own in time and space.

'. . . her ability to bring together ideas of poets, anthropologists, psychologists, psychoanalysts, philosophers and others makes the book fascinating reading' *The Times Literary Supplement*.